A Fishy Tale

Robert Kirk

Merlin Massara Publishing

First published in Great Britain by Merlin Massara Publishing in 2009

ISBN 9780954390020

All photographs and illustrations are from the author's personal collection,
some of which, due to their age and condition, are not easily traceable for ownership.
The Author and Publishers have made all reasonable efforts to clarify ownership of the
photographic images, however, if errors have been unintentionally made, owners are invited
to contact the publishers so that due acknowledgement can be given.

Typeset by Hope Services (Abingdon) Ltd.

Printed in Great Britain by the MPG Books Group, Bodmin and King's Lynn

Published By:
Merlin Massara Publishing
17 Tovey Close
London Colney
Hertfordshire
AL2 1LF. UK

The publishers are grateful to:
Alison Renshaw for reading and first editing.
Barbara James for second editing and proofreading.
Blackstar Studios, Chelmsford for photo restoration.
Paul Dunning for jacket design and layout.

I dedicate this book to the memory
of our dearly beloved grandson

Marc Ramsbotham

4th February 1973–8th June 2007

. . . missin' – gone fishin'!

Contents

I should perhaps start by apologising to my wife and daughters for the time I spent away from home pursuing my favourite hobby. Too much "missin' gone fishin'!"

Thanks to my old friend and ex-colleague, Ted Cheeseman, who prompted me to write these few lines.

Do not think I am name dropping on purpose—it was purely a matter of where I worked and lived.

Robert Kirk
June
2009

Chapter One

1924–1939
Early Memories and School Days

MY EARLIEST memories are of walking with my mother (in case I fell in) to our local River Hogsmill, which divided New Malden from Tolworth, complete with tupenny tiddler net and jam jar to catch sticklebacks. We used to walk through a meadow abounding with butterflies. They were nothing rare I later discovered mainly gatekeepers and meadow browns. The prize catch was a red throat—a male stickleback in full mating regalia. By all accounts the males build the nest on the river bottom and they even fan the eggs with their pectoral fins to supply the flow of water that is vital for a successful hatching. After that, they guard the eggs and young until they can fend for themselves.

I am afraid all this was turned into a concrete jungle long ago. However, it is still possible to walk from Kingston to Old Malden along the banks of the Hogsmill. Last year I had lunch at the Hogsmill pub and a party of hikers had just set off on the return trip. Judging by their walking poles, haversacks and heavy boots, they appeared more suited for an assault on the Himalayas than a riverside stroll!

With father's Bull Nose Morris, 1926.

My first real fishing came when I was about five years old. I went to stay with an aunt at her holiday cottage near Sudbury in Suffolk. This was one of a row of five or six and there was no gas, electricity or running water. Water had to be obtained from a deep well and cranked up by hand in a tin bucket before transferring it to your own container. The loo was outside and very much a 'bucket and chuck it' affair. Apart from these minor inconveniences, the cottages had all the latest mod cons! They must have been farm labourers' dwellings because I do not recall being even near a village. My aunt had an Austin 7 Ruby saloon, which shook and rattled on its merry way; that's when it didn't have a puncture, which happened nearly every day. How it made it from north London to Suffolk I'll never know. My aunt was an amazing woman as she was profoundly deaf and used one of the old-fashioned ear trumpets all the time, apart from when she was driving her little car. The vibration was the main cause of her deafness I would have thought. Despite this she taught elocution and one of her star pupils was the actress Dame Flora Robson.

Now for the fishing. During the first week of my holiday we went to Sudbury and I discovered the mill pool on the River Ouse. I did not have much in the way of tackle but made do with an ancient rod and reel and a cork float. I used bread paste made up of flour and water mixed to a stiff batter. This was before anyone thought of pinching a bit of bread flake onto the hook. I managed to catch a 4–5 inch roach, or it could have been a rudd, and was so delighted I insisted on having it cooked for breakfast next morning. Frankly I've never eaten anything so foul-tasting. Of course I had to say it was delicious!

A little later my father and mother took me to Egham on the River Thames. After a fruitless afternoon and while my parents were enjoying a cup of tea and cakes at a riverside café I found a small landing stage. By letting the float go with the flow, a practice known as long-trotting (although in my case it was more 'short trotting' owing to lack of line), I caught several small mottled fish on a worm and later found out they were gudgeon. I should have eaten them as according to Isaac Walton, author of *The Compleat Angler*, they are very good cooked in butter and tansy. What the hell is tansy? Probably some obscure herb. I'll have to ask Ike if I meet him on the banks of the Great Chalk Stream in the sky. On the other hand, I might not, as according to John Gierach, the American writer, he was a 'bank snoozer' and worm drowner. Apparently, Walton also had a great penchant for the milkmaids, their songs only, of course!

About this time my father bought me my first split cane rod and I was proud of it but I still did not have a decent reel. The rod cost the princely sum of ten shillings and sixpence, or fifty-two and a half pence if you prefer it. The next few years were spent fishing the River Thames, mainly for bleak. These are small,

Early days. Handline fishing from Seaview Pier, Isle of
Wight, 1930.

silvery fish that were once netted in quantity as their scales were used in the
manufacture of artificial pearls.

I was at King's College School in Wimbledon at the time and it was there,
when I was about fourteen years old, that I met John Beard. John, like me, was
crazy about fishing and wildlife. His father owned The Forrester's Arms pub on
Tooting Broadway which was a beer and wine pub only; no spirits were sold for
good reason. The clientele were rough, to say the least, and the place would soon
have been broken up. Every Friday night his mother used to stand at the window
throwing handfuls of florins and half-crowns to the waiting women in the street
below; their husbands having spent their wages on the way home! The Beards
lived above the pub and John had a pair of Australian stump-tail lizards that
roamed loose. He also had a bush baby, a crocodile which they kept in the living
room and heaven knows what else. I too bought a crocodile but kept mine in the
greenhouse well away from the house.

12lb Pike caught in King George VI Reservoir.

I did a lot of fishing with John and his father, mainly in the reservoirs near Molesey. We used to stop on the way to get our live bait and worms at a good tackle shop in Colliers Wood. We caught numerous perch, up to 1½ pounds and John eventually succeeded in catching a 5½ pound pike. We fished Frensham Great Pond, where there were perch under the moored punts and the three of us also had several sea trips out of Eastbourne. We would anchor about two miles off Beachy Head where the currents meet and it was very rough but we were rewarded with lots of tope up to 30 pounds and bull huss. That's when I found out what it was like to be really seasick. This was not helped by John's father, who would hang a whole York ham on the bone from the gunwale and cut slices off and eat them for hours on end, washed down with two or three bottles of best claret!

I remember my summer holidays well. My father sent John and I to a cricket school in Wandsworth run by Sandham, Strudwick and Gover, all County cricketers in the 1920s. My bowling was quite good but I wanted to brush up on my batting and poor John needed to learn just about everything—he wasn't good at sports. Fishing was, of course, an important summer activity as well. I now had a permit to fish the Royal Parks: Home, Bushy and Richmond. I used to cycle to the River Mole at East Molesey to get my live bait and then back to Home Park where I fished the Wall Pond (being nearest) and on occasion the Long Water. I rarely fished the Willow Pond. Again I caught small pike and perch.

John and I went to Belgium for a holiday with a French-speaking school master. He insisted on speaking French from the moment we got on the boat.

With my father, 1936.

What a disaster! I got by with 'oui' and 'non', which sufficed most of the time, as 'yes' and 'no' does in this country. We ended up in Dinant where we caught a lot of wall lizards on the rocks and fire salamanders on the plateaus. We also caught numerous swallowtail butterflies and John caught a Camberwell beauty, a very rare species. We fished the River Meuse and the feeder streams from a rowing boat, all without success until the last day when we managed to get some *asticots* (maggots, in English), and caught good roach below the main bridge.

September 3rd 1939 was my fifteenth birthday and also the day war broke out. Guess where I was—fishing! This time I was on the Thames at Kingston, below the railway bridge where the Hogsmill flows into the Thames. I was catching really good quality roach on hemp seed. About ten past eleven in the morning a

man came cycling down the towpath shouting "The war's started—take cover!"
I continued fishing and the air-raid sirens went off, closely followed by the all-clear. It was a false alarm caused by unidentified aircraft so I carried on fishing until it was time to go home.

About this time I updated my tackle, thanks to gifts of money for birthdays and other events. I bought a 7 foot split cane light casting rod, make unknown, and an Allcocks 'Flick-Em' centre pin reel. I learned to cast off the reel and as I had recently acquired a weir permit, I used to spin off the aprons on Molesey and Teddington weirs catching numerous small perch. I also purchased an Allcock 10 foot roach rod with two greenheart tops (a short one for ledgering which I never used) and an Aerialite reel made of Bakelite which was very good. I remember it was seven shillings and sixpence but I paid an extra shilling for a line guard!

I had another friend at school, John Burgess, whose parents had a house at Broomwater, which backed onto a tributary of the Thames just above Teddington Weir. I used to cycle down the towpath from Kingston and he would pick me up in the dinghy, complete with bike, and row me across to his house. Again we caught numerous perch trolling spinners by the moored boats. There was a boathouse below the weir that rented out moored punts. These were permanently moored by means of a long pole at each end across the current. They were secured by ropes and a large iron ring which slid up and down with the tide; Teddington being the last tidal weir on the Thames. The boathouse staff would row you out and pick you up later. I think it cost one shilling for an afternoon session. The poles were shod with an iron 'rye peck' which ended with a sharp double prong to cut through the gravel and mud. I still have one in my shed as a souvenir. It was great fun, particularly when they forgot to pick you up. The outbreak of war meant that my fishing was severely curtailed for the next few years.

It was exam time at King's and they were important ones, matriculation and school certificate. It was my intention to write this story in the order it happened but feel I must talk about my friend, John Beard. He was even worse at his studies than at sport. His parents employed two tutors to try and cram the knowledge into him and he was studying until late at night. Finally he broke down and threw all his books and papers out of the window before wrecking his room. He was eventually caught by the bar manager and to cut a long story short, he was sectioned. After being in various institutions he finished up in an asylum near Epsom. Later, when I was on embarkation leave for southern Rhodesia (Zimbabwe) I went to see him. When his minder said time was up, John said, "I want to go with him", pointing at me. His minder then said "You know what happened the last time you didn't do what you were told?" Poor John was led away in tears; he was eighteen.

A year later I returned from southern Rhodesia and called in on the Beards in Tooting. I was greeted with the sad news that John had died during the year. They said he had fallen down the stairs and hit his head, suffering a clot on the brain. You can form your own opinions about this, bearing in mind that a lot of the asylum inmates were hopeless cases and long-abandoned by their families. Also it was a self-contained unit and even had its own crematorium. I hate to think what happened when the minders returned after a night out on the beer. I am sorry to talk so much about my personal life instead of fishing but they are hopelessly intertwined, so that's it!

Exams were a worry for me as well. I was playing cricket for the school at the time and what with net practice every evening and matches at weekends there was little time for revision. However, I did manage school certificate, which says a lot for sport.

Chapter Two

1939–1941
The Second World War Begins

I DID NOT want to talk about the Second World War and I am only going to do so when relevant. In late August 1940, my father died as a direct result of enemy action. He was in the garden when a bomb dropped in the next road and the blast threw him up the back stairs, crushing his already weakened chest against a door. He died that same night. We immediately evacuated to my uncle's place, Wiremill House near Lingfield in Surrey. I can't think why it was thought to be safer than home as the Battle of Britain was in full swing and things were falling out of the sky in all directions.

In the middle of the Battle of Britain I was standing in the back yard of Wiremill House with George Rothwell, who was my uncle's gardener, chauffeur, come odd-job man, and Mr Thompson who rented an acre of land from uncle for market gardening. Mr Thompson only had his right arm, having had the left one blown off in the First World War. However, he still managed to dig the whole plot over using his right arm only and a leather loop around his neck. Mind you, his arm was about the same size as an average man's thigh. Anyway, suddenly a Heinkel III, the mainstream bomber of the Luftwaffe, came over very low, hotly followed by three Spitfires. The German plane was already hard hit and on fire. One of the Spits let off a burst of gunfire and hit a pile of coke that had been stacked outside ready for the Aga cooker. Lumps of coke flew in all directions. I had never heard language like Thompson used against the Germans; it was possible to be innocent at fifteen years of age in those far off days. Looking down I saw a .303 bullet from one of the Spitfires embedded in the tarmac only a few inches from my foot. I kept it as a souvenir. The Heinkel just cleared Woodcock Hill and before it crashed in a ball of fire on the outskirts of East Grinstead. Luckily no-one on the ground was injured. The following day I cycled up to New Malden to make sure Raleigh House was still standing and found a piece of meteorite on the tennis court. I have both items in my diddy box for posterity.

Wiremill House was only a few hundred yards from Hobbs Barracks, then occupied by the Canadian Army. 'Lord Haw-Haw', the pro-Nazi broadcaster noted this fact and the area was mentioned in one of his speeches on the BBC news. Sure enough, a few nights later we were firebombed though luckily no high explosives. After a hectic half an hour extinguishing the fires with handfuls of gravel and sand we turned our attention to the lake. The rushes were well alight in the surrounds and the fire brigade was in attendance. We were greeted with the astonishing sight of numerous foxes swimming in all directions in panic. They had obviously been after roosting wild fowl such as snipe and woodcock, which were there in abundance.

It was during my evacuation to Wiremill that I first met Ernie Borer, who was to become a lifelong friend. After sixty-seven years we still meet up regularly. We met in memorable circumstances. I shot a rabbit on his side of the dividing hedge and Ernie was in the field at the time and very kindly handed it to me. We just took it from there. I made quite a thing of shooting rabbits as I got one shilling each for them from the locals or one shilling and sixpence skinned, which was no problem to me. The proceeds enabled me to buy illicit cigarettes and kept me in cartridges. I also shot the occasional pheasant for the house. I didn't have a game licence as it was too expensive and come to think of it, I didn't even have a gun licence!

Now for the lake. My uncle had a punt moored in the rushes but it had been neglected for years and was half-sunk and rotten. The local Home Guard had criss-crossed the lake with wires to stop sea-planes landing—highly unlikely as it was only about two hundred yards long. However, they left behind an aluminium punt, 18 feet long by 4 feet. It was kept in an ancient boathouse and I made good use of it. However, I had no tackle at that time apart from an ancient bamboo rod of my uncle's which he used to poke out sparrows' nests from the gutters. It was not really a lot of good but I had my bike with me and so cycled up to Raleigh House, over twenty-five miles each way, to collect my own gear. It may seem a long way now but both Ernie and I did this many times and thought nothing of it. Back at Wiremill Lake I found an old paddle in one of the sheds and I was all set. Tackle was in short supply and I remember taking a rabbit snare apart to get a length of brass wire for pike fishing. Live bait was no problem as the lake was full of small rudd. I even made my own spoon by cutting off the handle of a dessert spoon and making a hole in each end. I wired a hook to one end and fashioned a wire loop at the other end of the line. It did not work like a commercially made spoon but laid on its convex side and wobbled. However it worked very well and caught very good perch and some small pike. If it was wet I would sit in the boathouse and catch small rudd which were there in abundance, like me they were keeping out of the rain!

There is a peculiar thing about Wiremill—down the lane lived a certain Bernard Venables who wrote the book *Fishing with Mr Crabtree*. This was fully illustrated and in 'strip cartoon' form. It covered most species and was a very popular read at five bob. At one London show a few years later, we sold over five hundred copies. The strange thing is he never fished the lake that was on his doorstep and I never heard of him fishing anywhere else come to that. Most odd.

Then it was back to Raleigh House and the nightly bombs. I was doing quite well at King's at that time and had the chance of a trial run with Surrey Colts cricket team, then based in Malden. My late dear father had entered me for a veterinary course at the Wye Agricultural College in Kent and I had been accepted. I was due to start in the autumn of 1942 but late that summer I decided to duck out altogether and instead went to work for Frazer Nash, a famous pre-war sports car manufacturer who was now making gun turrets. I think I went through every procedure at the factory, ending up on final test, which was to stand me in good stead later on.

About this time, I also joined the Air Raid Precautions Wardens (ARP) as a messenger, riding my bike. The idea was to put the bike in the transport when there was an incident so you could form a communication with base and the other services. Although I was still young, I was determined to contribute to the war effort.

Chapter Three

1941–1942
Joining the RAF

AS SOON as I was seventeen and a quarter years old, the minimum age, I volunteered for the RAF. I went in as aircrew although I could not be called up for another year. All the lads in my road were waiting to go into the various services or were already in. That is, apart from Gordon Boxall who was a conscientious objector, or 'conchie' for short. He got so much stick from the rest of us that he eventually volunteered for the RAF providing he was put on air-sea rescue launches. He was accepted on those terms and spent the war fishing downed aircrew out of the Channel, a very rewarding occupation.

I volunteered in Kingston and was sent to Croydon for the preliminary medical and then to Weston-super-Mare for assessment and full medical, which was very strict. At lunchtime we went on the pier and the attendant very kindly switched on the dodgem cars for us and we spent a happy half hour on them for free. Then it was back to the medical. I have heard the following story on the wireless since but for me it was absolutely true. The doctor asked us to pass urine in one of the small bottles on the shelf and one of our number, who no doubt, had been told of how fit you had to be to pass the medical asked "What? From here?" That, along with the sight of several men who couldn't go at all and were drinking pints of water and jogging round the yard to the sound of a running tap, made my day.

There was little time for fishing owing to war work and duties in the ARP. I was exactly eighteen and a quarter when I was called up and told to report to No 1 Aircrew Receiving Centre, then at Lords' Cricket Ground, St John's Wood. On arrival I was greeted with the sight of a long wooden railing in front of the Long Room—no doubt for the Members to lean on when they were too pissed to stand after too many large G&T's. On this rail was pinned a notice saying 'Hitching rail for canteen cowboys'. I found out what that meant a little later. After kitting out we were marched to Seymour Hall, a luxury block of flats in St John's Wood. We had our food in the old restaurant in London Zoo—we probably looked like a lot of monkeys. I no longer thought of mealtimes, seeing them rather as feeding times!

Breakfast was at 7 a.m. and after that is was marching. As it was still dark the front rank had to carry white paraffin lanterns and the rear rank had red ones. Our corporal, Corporal Fox, marched in safety on the pavement! We then found out the meaning of that notice at Lords' as one day we were marched round the block and brought to a halt outside a Salvation Army canteen. Corporal Fox said "Before I dismiss you to the canteen you lot can buy me a large kawfee an' fhree h'eccles cakes". Another time we were marching down the road and passed a bus stop with a large queue. A newly commissioned second lieutenant (Army) shouted out "Corporal, where are your men's eyes?" no doubt expecting a salute from Foxie and an 'eyes left' from us. One of our number shouted back, "In their bloody heads, of course!" He chased us up the road all to no avail. I am pleased to say he missed his bus.

Then it was embarkation leave and home for Christmas. It was unclear where we were going to be posted as alternate drafts went to Canada or Africa. However, we were left in no doubt where we were headed when we were issued with tropical kit as well as flying kit which gave us three kitbags to carry instead of the normal one—charming.

Embarkation leave 1942.

Chapter Four

1943
Intensive Training in Africa

W E WERE then posted to Blackpool to await the ship. The digs were not good, a boarding house on the front. We were paraded on the seafront at 9 a.m. and dismissed just fifteen minutes later with nothing to do until the next day. What do you do on two shillings a day? We could not go back to the billet except for meal times, so had to amuse ourselves as best we could. Luckily both Blackpool Tower and dance floor, the Zoo and the Winter Gardens only charged sixpence admission. After a fortnight of this we were moved just down the road to Morecombe. Happily, conditions were much better. Comfortable digs, good food and the landlady had a lovely daughter.

After a week or so in Morecombe, we finally moved to Liverpool to board the S.S. *Otranto*—an Orient Line ship. Conditions were terrible; overcrowded and not enough food. We formed a three-line convoy in the outer Channel and set off round the north coast of Ireland in a force ten gale. It was so rough that the ship abreast of us, the *Empress of Scotland*, hastily renamed from the *Empress of Japan* for obvious reasons, was completely disappearing in the massive wave troughs. She was a big ship by any standards but only the tips of her masts were visible. A Condor, a German long-range spotting plane, constantly tracked us. He kept well out of range of the escorts' AA fire but I wondered where the RAF was. After we turned south round the tip of Ireland it was obvious where we were heading and we saw no more of the Condor. All went well until approaching Gibraltar, when the port column of the convoy broke away to go into the Straits. Unfortunately for them a U-boat pack was waiting and many ships were lost. I had an army friend on one who escaped the carnage; I heard all about it from him when we shared a drink on embarkation leave. He landed safely in North Africa only to be killed shortly afterwards.

Our onward journey took us to Freetown in Sierra Leone, where we stopped briefly to take on more troops, which added to the overcrowding. It was now so hot we'd taken to sleeping on deck. We were carrying several tons of Cadbury's chocolate that started to melt so they sold it off at a farthing a bar. I was so hungry that I was eating six bars before breakfast! After six weeks at sea, in an eight-knot convoy (the speed of the slowest ship) and slowed further by zigzagging to fool the U-boats, we finally docked in Durban. We were transferred to Clairwood Camp, a vast place that held up to 10,000 men in transit.

On visiting the Airmen's Mess for the first time I was greeted by an old school friend who was serving the food; it turned out he was en route to India. After rationing in England and our privations on the ship, I could not believe the tables piled high with butter and two-pound tins of jam. We stayed at Clairwood for a fortnight or so. Every afternoon the women from Durban would park their damn great American cars at the gates ready to take you into town, for swimming, or whatever you fancied!

The ablutions were worthy of note. They were about fifty yards long and started with a laundry where you could do your own washing. You had to as there were no other facilities. Then there was a washing and shaving area, followed by open air showers and finally the toilets. These consisted of about one hundred paving slabs with holes in the middle in two rows so it was definitely a back-to-back and cheek-to-cheek job. No time for false modesty! There was a large concrete trough running under the complex to take away the waste. This worked well as water was running from about 6 a.m. until late at night. Some wags used to bundle up newspapers and set light to them before floating them under the toilets. You can imagine what happened!

After a fortnight in camp we were taken by train to Bulawayo, southern Rhodesia (now Zimbabwe). This was a two-day and one-night trip; four men to a compartment with two drop-down bunks over the seats which doubled as beds. My main memories are of the daylight stops when all the local ladies would turn out with tables laden with food and all sorts of goodies. The locals certainly looked after us. On arrival in Bulawayo we were marched up to Hillside Camp. This was a former cattle market and we were billeted in the cattle sheds. There was a big gap between the roof and the walls, which were made of double-skinned canvas stuffed with straw; this proved to be was an ideal habitat for snakes, as we soon found out. And so started eight weeks of intensive training, which covered all subjects from map reading to navigation. We used to parade at 7 a.m. marching past the Standard to the sounds of the RAF march played on a gramophone. The CO took the salute. Then it was breakfast and straight to lectures. Every couple of weeks we were put on perimeter guard and each man had about two hundred yards to patrol. We were not armed so we would have been pretty useless if attacked. The shifts were two hours on and four hours off. More interesting than guard duty were the *bhundu* (bush) bashes. We started with a compass and did short exercises of about one hundred yards. The training climaxed with being taken out in the dead of night in a truck and dumped at intervals, miles from camp. The object location was usually a farm, about ten

Black Mamba. Bulawayo 1943.

miles from the drop-off point. On arrival, once again, we were given a warm welcome. We saw plenty of buck and ostriches, but luckily no lions as again we were unarmed. One morning a chap discovered a snake under his bed, species unknown. We beat it to death and later discovered it was a black mamba, one of the most deadly snakes in Africa. Their bite can kill a human in hours.

Whilst at Hillside we met a couple who lived nearby and three of us, Dave King, Wally Hansley and myself, used to stay with them on Saturday nights on special pass from camp. I managed to borrow some tackle and fished in the Matopos Dam. This is in the Matopos Hills and below where Cecil Rhodes, the founder of Rhodesia, lies in a grave hewn out of solid rock—no doubt to stop people getting at him. Rorke's Drift and all that! Incidentally, the grandparents of one of the couple we met came up from South Africa with Rhodes. Using some odd, local insects for bait, I caught some small eel-like fish that nobody knew the name of.

Now it was time for final exams at Hillside and only forty per cent passed. Those who failed were moved on to other postings but those of us who did pass had a few days leave. A small party of us travelled up to the Victoria Falls. I was very keen to do this because of my Great Aunt Clemmie, who lived with us at Raleigh House (she was bedridden and died at a great age in the 1930s). Her cousin was the great journalist and explorer Sir Henry Morton Stanley of Stanley and Livingstone fame. Apparently, when I was five or six, I used to sit and talk with her for hours on end. She was a great artist and I still have a few of her miniature watercolours and her original folding artists' chair. I suppose I am a very distant relative of the great man himself, so that visit to the Falls was special for me.

It was a great trip and the River Zambezi was in full flood so the view was amazing. We stayed at the Falls Hotel at a very low price—enjoying the discount given to the Forces. I'd hate to think what it would cost now. I believe that these

The Round House Hotel outside Bulawayo, S. Rhodesia, 1943.

Cecil Rhodes' grave at World's View, Matopos Hills, 1943.

Matopos Dam June 1943, seen at 6a.m. on the 10 mile 'bhundu bash'.

Shabami, Southern Rhodesia, 1943.

days they have jet boats going through the spray and even bungee jumping from the top of the Falls. I did see a couple of locals spinning in the rapids and catching tiger fish which looked to me to be in the 2–3 pound class.

On my return to Hillside I was posted to No. 26 Elementary Flying Training School (EFTS) at Guinea Fowl, near Gwelo. Our day started at 6 a.m. with 'gunfire', which was a mug of tea and a currant bun. Then it was off to the flights. Our first job was to get the aircraft out of the hangars. They were so light that this was done by grabbing the tailplane struts, lifting and then walking them out. The idea was to get the flying done before it got too hot and the 'dust devils' appeared in numbers. These were mini whirlwinds, about three feet high, quite harmless to humans but capable of turning a Tiger Moth over if they got under the wing.

My first instructor was a Sergeant Kemm. In my opinion, we seemed to spend too much time sitting on the field and watching the secretary birds landing instead of flying ourselves. He kept saying "Do as they do". After six hours with him I was not making much progress. Most pupils went solo in ten to twelve hours; if you got to fourteen hours you were automatically scrubbed. So I changed instructors to a Flight Lieutenant Gordon and soloed in three hours and so beat them all! What a nice man he was. He lived off camp, on a large rented farm, with his lovely Egyptian wife. Our first job in the morning was to fly over his place and drop off the previous day's newspapers. Better late than never. Often, at weekends, he would invite me over to his farm and we would shoot baboons that were raiding his mealie crops. Back in the cockpit, I did quite a few hours solo and even passed the Chief Flying Instructor's test.

My first solo was quite eventful. It was the best experience of my life and I remember singing my head off on the circuit. That is, until I came in to land when I undershot the runway badly. I opened the throttle and then overshot and so had to go round again. No singing this time as I was concentrating on getting the bloody thing back on the ground in one piece, as well as myself! My instructor, who was waiting, said "I hope you enjoyed that, because I didn't". Then came the crunch. I failed the 'link' to move up to Harvards. It was blacked so you had to 'fly' on instruments which I had never seen before. So I was scrubbed as a pilot and was posted to Morpeth in Northumberland to re-muster as an air gunner. So I then had to do the whole trip in reverse.

I spent another two weeks in Durban before boarding the *Nieuw Amsterdam*. She was the flagship of the Dutch Mercantile Marine and had been mothballed in Sydney until Churchhill ruled that as the Dutch were our allies she must be used as a troopship. This time there were no convoys, no escorts and no zigzagging, so progress was much faster. After a brief stop in Cape Town for repairs, it was straight into the middle of the Atlantic and full speed for home.

We then got a new bomb aimer by the name of Lou Jevons who turned out to be brilliant and not only as a bomb aimer. We actually won the group practice bombing exercise which took place over the Yorkshire moors. It was my job in tail turret to unstrap myself, open the turret doors and lean out to spot the bombs' point of impact. You could easily become another bomb! Lou had two regular girlfriends and after a short leave he learned they were both pregnant. Some going on a forty-eight hour pass!

We then converted from Wellingtons to Lancasters at 1651 Heavy Conversion Unit (HCU) Woolfox Lodge on the old A1, north of Grantham in Lincolnshire. This was a short, uneventful course. Our huts were two miles from the Mess and we were issued with bikes. Luckily there was a 'greasy spoon' café much closer where you could get a full breakfast for one shilling and sixpence, so we used it quite often. I also remember walking through the woods and finding a small lake which was alive with good carp. One night we got out to the kite and before take-off the sound of four Merlins running up was drowned out by nightingales singing. There must have been over fifty of them, all trying to outdo the Lancasters. By Merlins, I don't mean the birds of that name but the Lancaster engines.

Chapter Six

1944–1946
218 Squadron

AFTER HCU we were posted to No 218 Gold Coast Squadron. This was a fantastic outfit and today, is one of the squadrons which has an Association. The annual reunion has been in operation for the past fifteen years and lasts three days. In recent years, we have gone down for the Sunday service round the war memorial on the green at Chedburgh in Suffolk followed by lunch and a get-together. It was at Chedburgh that I first met Roland Bishop. We both shared a love of motorbikes and, at that time, he was the proud owner of a Triumph Speed Twin. This was a rarity indeed, apart from those assigned to the 'speed cops' who used them all the time. Roland was to play a big part in my life later on.

Outside 218 Squadron Church at Chedburgh, July 1995.

Self and Edna. Just off to 218
Squadron reunion at
Chedburgh, July 1996.

On arrival at 218, our navigator Ken Jones, our mid upper gunner and I were sent to Feltwell, Norfolk on a week's course. Ken was to learn the GH mouse (radar) and we two gunners were sent to master the new gyro gun sight. Meanwhile the rest of the crew 'borrowed' replacements for the three of us and did a proving cross-country. On arrival back at Chedburgh it was our turn and we were detailed to go on a cross-country exercise to the north of Scotland. Our pilot was ex-University Air Squadron. At briefing the Met Officer said we were to expect stratus clouds up to 10,000 feet, but there could be cumulus nimbus pouring through it. We were told that, if we preferred, we could go the day after instead, as there was no point in risking a good aircraft—never mind about us!

However, our pilot then said in his plumy voice; "OK chaps, we'll go". All went well until we got to the Mull of Kintyre, when we flew straight into a 'cunim'. We were struck by lightning, rendering the wireless useless and were caught in a down-draught, losing several thousand feet and nearly turning over. The Lanc is a big aeroplane, with a 102 foot wingspan! Luckily our navigator was on the ball and got us safely down on the ground at Jurby on the Isle of Man. We stayed the night before returning to Chedburgh the next day. The three of us had a hell of a night in Douglas, and blow the rest of the crew!

Now, a bit more about the Lancaster which was the best heavy bomber of the Second World War. It was excellent at high altitude; we normally flew at 18,000–20,000 feet. It was also very effective at ground level—as demonstrated so impressively by The Dambusters, 617 Squadron, in the raids on the Ruhr Dams. They were led, famously, by Wing Commander Guy Gibson VC and

Lovely Lou and crew, Chedburgh 1944/5. From left to right:

Bob Kirk—rear gunner. Lou Jevons—bomb aimer. George Martin—flight engineer. Georg Maybury—skipper (pilot). Ken Jones—navigator. Bryn Parfit—wireless operator. Ray Taylor—mid upper gunner.

armed with Barnes Wallis's bouncing bomb. The normal version of the Lancaster could carry up to a 10,000 lb bomb. It was also well armed and carried eight .303 Browning machine guns of which the bomb aimer, who doubled as a front gunner, had two; the mid-upper gunner also had two; and myself, as rear gunner, had four. The very latest Lancs had a hole cut in the floor and a swivel-mounted .5 Browning, enabling it to be fired downwards. This was to combat the German Focke-Wulf 190's which now had two upward firing cannon mounted behind the cockpit, the idea being to fly underneath you and blow you out of the sky. It was said that the German pilots would claim five or six kills before landing to refuel and re-arm. Luckily none of 218 Squadron was affected.

The Lanc was also a good long distance plane. Before my time the Squadron raided Milan in Italy before flying on to North Africa to refuel and re-arm, the idea being to drop a few more bombs on the way home! Unfortunately Flight Sergeant Aaron was seriously wounded by Italian 'flak'. The crew got to North Africa where Aaron insisted on landing the kite himself as there was no other pilot on board. He died soon afterwards and was awarded the VC posthumously. The Lancastrian, the civil version of the Lancaster, flew from London to Cairo non-stop and both the Aga Khan and the entertainer George Formby used it en route to South Africa—more of that later.

My lasting memory of the Lancaster is of it performing a low level fly past in 2002 over The Marquis, 218's local pub at Chedburgh. I was pleased that my wife Edna and daughters, Gill and Sue, were with me to witness it. We could hear the growl of the engines long before it came into sight, barely missing the trees and telephone wires. It flew past at around one hundred feet and dipped its wings in salute to us. A truly wonderful sight and there were a lot of wet eyes amongst us.

After the war in Europe was won, we went onto manna trips, dropping food to the starving Dutch. They were called manna after the 'bread from heaven' referred to in the Bible. This was low level stuff, which the mad Aussie pilots tackled with reckless exuberance. There were stories of them bending the tips of their propellers by hitting the waves in the North Sea on the way over. It got so bad that they put RAF police on board the flights just to put an end to it. The crews replied by flying at a reasonable height and flinging the kites around, which soon rendered the police useless for anything.

After this we operated as a forward attack squadron and joined the newly formed 'Tiger Force' to fight the Japanese. We made quite a few low level training trips over the Wash, off Hunstanton. At our first briefing the gunnery office instructed us to concentrate on small red buoys; also saying "You will also probably see some black ones bobbing about, they'll be seals so have a pop at them as well". Imagine the outcry these days!! Actually, I didn't see any, but probably accounted for a few low-flying seagulls.

At this time, we were co-operating with the USAAF, who were flying Mustangs. They came in so close that you could almost touch the spinners on their propellers—they were some pilots! We were told that we were to be based in mainland China for low level raids on Japan—presumably low level to get under the Jap radar. We were also to be issued with a cyanide capsule before every 'op' in case we crashed and survived. It was to be taken before the Japanese, notorious for their cruel treatment of POWs, got to us and subjected us to torture. Although the consequences were horrific, I must admit we were very glad when the Yanks ended Japanese resistance by dropping the atomic bombs on Hiroshima and Nagasaki.

Another significant, and now historically controversial, episode in the wartime work of the Lancaster concerns the raid on Dresden in 1945. You would think that by now this action could be consigned to the past, but no, someone had to dig it all up again recently. To me he did not sound old enough to even remember the Second World War; even so, he accused those air crews involved of mass murder. The first thing to consider is the context: Dresden was a hugely significant industrial target. It's factories were turning out armaments and communications equipment and it formed a bridge between East and West in Europe. It is well known that the death toll in Dresden was very high but it should be remembered that heavy losses were also sustained by Bomber Command during the war—some 55,500 lives lost.

When we arrived above Dresden in the second wave the master bomber was calling out, "Bomb on red," meaning that we were to aim at the red flares he had dropped. However, the whole city was ablaze and even the worst bomb aimer could not have missed it. The heat was so intense that even at our altitude we were bouncing about like a pea on a drum. Each aircraft carried 1,000 incendiaries plus a 4,000 pound 'cookie' to make sure the fires spread. I remember it was a damn long trip there and even more so coming back.

Of course, we regretted the civilian losses, but at the time we felt there was a lot of truth in the old saying 'An eye for an eye and a tooth for a tooth'. Remember the raids on Warsaw, Rotterdam, London, Coventry and all the other cities. Apart from my father being killed in the first daylight raid on London, a V-I Buzz Bomb landed in our road destroying a house and killing two friends of ours. Raleigh House was badly damaged and the garage fell in, almost destroying a brand new Wolseley 14/60, which my father had bought in 1939 and had hardly used because of petrol rationing.

So that was the end of it all. The Squadron was immediately disbanded and many of us were re-trained as ground staff and sent overseas to relieve those who had served their time.

Chapter Seven

1945–1946
Africa Again—The RAF After the War

W E WERE first sent to Burn in Yorkshire for selection, and I was then posted to Preston for a course on storemanship, of all things. After a few weeks I passed that and was posted to Palestine, which meant another sea trip. I was getting more sea hours in than the average sailor. This time we sailed on the *Capetown Castle* from Southampton. After an uneventful passage we landed at Alexandria and transferred to Almaza, a transit camp outside Cairo. This was a large bell-tented camp and the day before I was due to leave for Palestine, I tripped over a tent peg and sprained my ankle. I was unable to go and instead was re-located to go to Kenya, this time I was to be in charge of catering, something I knew nothing about.

As ships were scarce and planes even more so, I travelled in luxury on a 'C' class flying boat—the civil version of the Sunderland. By amazing coincidence, I found myself sitting next to my neighbour from New Malden! He was a big noise in the railway police and was on his way to South Africa to advise them on new methods. After stops at Luxor, Khartoum (overnight), and Port Bell at the top end of Lake Victoria, we finally arrived at Kisumu at the other end of the lake. Before every take-off we were preceded by a fast motor launch to clear the water of any hippos or crocodiles. I disembarked at Kisumu and was immediately flown on to

Self at Kisumu, 1946.

Nairobi, only to be told there was a mistake and I was to be flown back to Kisumu straight away.

At the aerodrome, the sight of glistening silver Skymaster greeted me. At about this time the flying boats were being taken over by Skymasters, an American plane flown by South Africans. I knew that they landed at Kisumu, so was excited at the thought of flying in one. However, my hopes were dashed when suddenly a little twin-engined Anson taxied out. This was the type of plane I had graduated on as an air gunner. There was only the pilot and myself on board so I sat in the jump seat. When I asked what happened if we had to make a forced landing, he replied "Stay where we are and hope there are no lions about!"

Back at Kisumu I reported to the CO, a mere Flying Officer, the same rank as my skipper on Lancs. He asked me if I could drive, as I was no good to him if I couldn't because he had no spare driver for me. Before I joined the RAF I had learnt to drive and had a full licence (I never took a test in my life!), so I said yes, but my licence was in England. He said "That's good enough" and I was 'issued' with a damn great big Dodge 3-tonner. I was to use this to collect the rations from the market and I could also use it as personal transport, which was very handy. Believe me, it did quite a few miles!

After a crash course of a week with Sergeant Taylor, the man I was relieving, I was on my own. Before he left I bought his .256 Mannlicher rifle, which was very high-powered and good at extreme range. I used it to shoot crocs near the

My personal transport—
3 ton Dodge. Kisumu 1945.

An alternative transport—
3 ton Ford. Kisumu 1946.

Alternative transport!!

'Boxer'. Our police dog, June 1946.

abattoir. They weren't that big, all around four to five feet, but I did get one of about fifteen feet from the RAF launch on a day out. I gave it to the Indians to be turned into shoes and handbags. Apart from this, I shot the odd gazelle for the Sergeants' Mess and several hyenas, which were raiding the rubbish bins at night.

I met two people of note in Kisumu. One was the Aga Khan III, a huge man, on his way to Dar-es-Salaam to be weighed in diamonds to mark his Diamond Jubilee. He had already done a gold weigh-in in 1937 to mark his Golden Jubilee and the money raised was used for social welfare projects. He paid for all we RAF bods to have a meal at the hotel, which I'm sure, hardly dented his coffers.

The second famous person I met was George Formby. He was on his way to South Africa, as the dry air was recommended for his consumption. I happened to be down at the 'drome when he and his wife were waiting to board their plane. He got talking to me and we took each other's photos. What a nice man he was.

The Ration Staff. Kisumu June 1946.

George Formby and his wife boarding a Skymaster Tafelburg.

He was saying what a wonderful place Blackpool was, what with the Tower and Ballroom, Winter Gardens and so on. I said that might be so, but it was still a bloody awful place to be stationed in! We had a good laugh about that.

There was a small RAF camp at Entebbe, about two hundred miles away, which closed down and a group of us had to go up and collect their transport. Why they could not drive it down themselves, I'll never know. Among the various vehicles there was a 350 cc BSA motorbike. Believe it or not, out of the fifty or so men on camp, I was the only person who had ridden one. I said "Chuck it in the back of one of the lorries", but no, they told me my job was to ride at the back of the convoy. If there was a breakdown I was to ride up to the front of the convoy and stop it so that we would not get fragmented.

On the way back, we had a small drama with the water bowser. The driver was told to empty the water out as we didn't think he would get up the escarpment with a full load. He got up all right, but it transpired he had only let about half the water out. Coming down the other side, which was quite steep, the water started to swill about as there were no baffles in the tank. He got into an uncontrollable steering wobble and went over the side finishing up in the valley below. Luckily, he managed to jump out before it picked up speed. We left the bowser where it was; the driver was more concerned about the fags he'd left in the cab than the vehicle.

About this time we laid on a grand dance in the Sergeants' Mess to celebrate the first anniversary of VE day. All the local dignitaries came, including Lady Bowes-Lyon, a cousin of the Queen Mother. Elvis Presley was all the rage at the time and I had a pair of blue suede shoes made by an Indian cobbler. I thought I'd look the bee's knees, until I found that my personal boy had found them under my bed, and trying to be helpful, had tried to polish them with black boot polish! Apart from that life in Kisumu went on as usual. You have probably seen the film, or read the book *White Mischief.* Well that's what it was like, and me with my own transport. That's enough said about that!

I played rugby for the station. We did not have much success, as Kisumu was more or less at sea level and most of our matches were in the highlands.

Sergeant's Mess at Kisumu. Ready for the Victory Day Anniversary Dance, 1946.

Sergeant's Mess, Kisumu, 1945.

Entebbe, for instance, was 8,000 feet above sea level and after one run down the pitch, you were knackered and unable to breathe. We were playing against coffee planters who had probably been born there and were used to such rarefied air.

One of the things worthy of note in Kisumu was the fishing; Lake Victoria was full of tilapia, or more commonly called, lake fish. They are the best tasting fish I have ever eaten, including all the English species. They told me they could not be caught, only netted, as they were plankton feeders. However, I had some hooks sent down from Nairobi, got some strong thread from one of the local cobblers and made a pole up from bamboo. For bait I used a paste made up of *pojo*, mealie meal, or ground maize and water, which was the staple native diet in those days, except they mixed it with *ghee* (clarified butter), rolled it into balls and dipped it in fresh blood. Lunch anyone? Anyway, it worked and I caught several tilapia, all about 1½ pounds.

I was watching the Great North Run on television recently and noted that one chap was running for a charity called 'The Street Children of Kisumu'. When I was there it had one main street, a hotel, an air strip and the RAF camp. All the other roads were earth, or had two macadam strips if you were lucky. I suppose after exactly sixty years there had to be some improvement. It sounds as if it is a teeming city now, something I find hard to imagine.

In November 1946 my de-mob came up and I was not sure what to do as I was having an affair with the daughter of the owner of the Kisumu Hotel and had the offer of becoming assistant manager. Also, a South African friend, Yanni Pietrie, wanted me to join him as a white hunter with a safari outfit he was starting. However, my mother was unwell, so I decided to return to England. So it was goodbye to Kisumu and after a one-night stop in Nairobi we arrived in Mombassa to get the boat home.

In Mombassa, there were several wooden compounds outside the camp containing various animals awaiting trans-shipment to zoos around the world. There were kudu and many other antelopes and gazelle, also ostriches and even warthogs. I remember thinking "Make the most of the African sun, because heaven knows where you'll finish up". Poor little devils; destined to be behind bars for the rest of their lives. One night a lion entered the camp and after a brief look round left by the same way it came in. By the way, there were no predators, leopards or cheetahs, and obviously no lions in the cages. The latter roamed loose. Probably looking for an easy meal in the compounds!

After a fortnight in Mombassa we embarked for home at last. By coincidence, the ship was the S.S. *Orantes*, the sister ship of the *Otranto*, the ship on which I first sailed to Africa. We sailed north up the Red Sea, through the Suez Canal, then across the Med to Gibraltar and finally to Liverpool, the home port of the Orient Line. This meant that I had completely circumnavigated Africa, apart from the small stretch of ocean between Durban and Mombassa.

On board ship, I met a Flight Lieutenant who had been an educational officer in Kenya. He had heard that jobs were scarce in England but reckoned he would be OK as he could go back to teaching. He asked me what I had done pre-war and all I could think of was assembling and testing FN4 gun turrets for Lancasters. He didn't think that would be much good. However, I did have my school certificate, which was also to prove useless!

Chapter Eight

1947–1960

Civvie Life—Beginning in the Fishing Tackle Trade

AFTER MUCH trying for various jobs I finally landed one through a friend with a plastics firm in Walthamstow. This meant a long journey for me but it was worth it. I was what they called a 'progress chaser'. My job was to trace the progress of the firm's goods through the factory. Our office manager was a chap called Gude, and what an idiot he was. He was always on the 'phone. "Gude speaking—that's spelt George, Uncle, Dog and Edward." He had been some minor rank in the Navy but behaved like a Vice Admiral. Luckily I made friends with the export manager and we shared motorbikes, thus saving rationed petrol for our cars. Many of the rest of the men were typical of those who had avoided wartime service for reasons best known to themselves. One great blob of a man sticks in my mind. I was there nearly a year and never did find out what work he actually did. I don't think he knew either! I really hated it; the only good thing that came out of working there was meeting my beloved wife, Edna, who worked in the same office.

By the time Edna and I were engaged I had got a job, through a doctor friend of mine, in a garage. It was at a service station on Clapham Common and I was doing minor repairs. I had a lock-up iron bench out in the open, which was continually being broken into so I learnt not to take my own tools to work. Although the new job wasn't ideal, it had been a pleasure to give my notice in to the beloved Gude! From the Clapham Common job I moved to the Acorn Service Station on the Kingston by-pass, within walking distance of my house, which made a nice change. It was there that I met Ken Tully who was to become a lifelong friend and with whom I'm still very much in touch. Then I moved again, this time just up the road to Meeten's, a motorcycle firm. It suited me better as I preferred bikes to cars and Edna also got a job there as secretary to the bosses.

It was whilst I was at Meeten's that I answered an advert placed by Hardy Brothers of Alnwick for a salesman at their main branch in Pall Mall. They were the finest rod makers in the world at the time. I had to have two interviews, as at the first one they did not reckon I knew enough about trout or salmon. This was true as I had only caught a few small trout on the worm in the small Sussex streams. Hastily, I borrowed some books from the library and passed on the second attempt, landing the job.

On reporting to Pall Mall I was told that I was to re-open their City branch in the Royal Exchange. The manager was Tom Parry, an older man, who had spent the war years in the stores department at the factory in Alnwick. What he had done there I do not know. I discovered later that they had only made bamboo scaling ladders for the Commandos and split oak and bamboo telephone posts for the Signals Corps. I also soon realised that he knew even less about trout fishing than I did. Our first job was to go down the road to Moss Bros to be measured for the standard company dress. This was a black jacket and waistcoat and pinstripe trousers, so we looked pretty smart. After a couple of hectic weeks unpacking boxes of rods and other tackle, we were ready to open up the shop once again.

I had several customers of note. Lord Ashburton, who fished the lower River Itchen, purchased a No 2 LR Hardy spinning rod and Elarex spinning reel. I remember this well as it was the first 'class outfit' that I sold. He had to wait for the reel as components were in short supply after the war. I got to thinking and remembered that whilst at King's College School and in the Officers' Training Corps, I had been in the team that had shot for the Ashburton Cup at Bisley. This was .303 full-bore stuff shot over fifty to one hundred yards. We had actually won it! When his Lordship came in to collect his reel I mentioned this to him; he was really interested and we had a good chat. He was a pleasant and decent man and it was a great pity he was mixed up with the Baring Bank collapse in 1995. After he left the shop Tom called me to one side and told me that I was not supposed to engage titled people in conversation. I explained the situation; in response he said "Hmph" and walked away!

While at Hardy's City branch, Edna and I had a holiday on the east coast of Scotland, at a place called Inverbervie. We stayed at the Castle Hotel, which was about one hundred yards from the River Bervie. It was cold in the hotel and poor Edna was not allowed in the bar; in those days it was men only. She spent her time in our room crying and reading while I went night fishing for small sea trout, about 8–12 ounce on fly, with a maggot on the hook. They were called herling or finnock locally. On the Saturday night I was fishing on my own, which was unusual. Suddenly a deep Scottish voice behind me said "There's nae fishing on the Sabbath". It was the local bailiff; I then realised it was ten past midnight. He wanted to confiscate my tackle but after I pleaded ignorance I got away with it.

On our way home to Surrey we stopped off at Alnwick, the headquarters of Hardy Brothers situated in 'Bondgate Without'. We were treated like royalty as we were the only people from their numerous branches who had bothered to call. Probably we were the only folk with a car. We met Laurie Hardy, the overall boss, who had many rods named after him. He was a short and very rotund man and he remembered me from his visit to the City branch when I took his arm, helped him across the road and hailed a taxi for him. He was renowned for being useless in city traffic.

The company secretary took us on a tour of the works, which was amazing. The only section we were not allowed to see was the cane splitting room, which was top secret. You have to remember that they listed sixty plus rods in their catalogue, many with optional lengths; also all three-piece trout and salmon fly rods had two tops, so it was quite an operation. We were allowed to see the straightening process where the section was slapped down hard on the flat sides on a sheet of marble. There were five or six men employed in the factory who took a turn each for one hour only as that was as long as your eyes would hold up to the strain. We were then treated to a slap-up meal at yet another Castle Hotel and booked in for the night, another first for Hardy's. It was lovely and warm and that's where Gill's life started!

Back at the shop, another customer of note was Field Marshall Viscount Alanbrooke, who had water on the middle River Kennet. When he came into the shop, he told me that the fish were not actually rising to the fly but swirling just below the surface. As a dry fly purist, fishing upstream, he could not bring himself to fish the wet fly downstream, not that he owned any wet patterns! Luckily I had recently read Skue's book on upstream nymph fishing, and as we had his patterns in stock, I hastily sold the Viscount a selection. I advised him to grease the cast down to the last two inches so the nymph would fish just below the surface. He came back a few days later and told me he had caught several good fish and was delighted with me. He was a member of the Zoological Society of London and invited Edna and I, now married, to go with him on a Sunday morning to London Zoo. It was closed to the public then and, as private guests, we could go behind the scenes in all the animal houses. Unfortunately I could not accept his invitation as Edna was close to giving birth to our daughter, Gillian.

It was whilst working in the City branch of Hardy Brothers that I first met Mr Burt. He was a buyer and seller of second-hand Hardy tackle, who I was to be lumbered with for years to come. Around this time I also met John Birth, who was then working across the road in the Stock Exchange; I helped him out with some rod bits from my own collection. Not long afterwards, he became the manager of Enton Lakes, a trout fishing complex near Godalming, Surrey. He lived in a bungalow on site owned by his former boss at the Stock Exchange.

I had another friend, Bill Chivers, who worked in Hardy's main branch in Pall Mall. He used to help me out in the City when Tom Parry was ill or on holiday.

John Birth invited us both down for a day on Enton Lakes. There were three lakes: the upper and lower by the bungalow and the large lake, which was on the far side of the main Waterloo to Portsmouth railway. We fished from a punt, which was quite luxurious with fully rotating armchairs so you could fish in any direction. Both Bill and I caught small rainbow trout of about one pound in weight. By this time I had purchased a Hardy Triumph 8 foot 9 inch split cane rod and 3⅛ Uniqua reel, the cheapest in their range. With staff discount they still cost me nine pounds, which was quite a lot in those days especially as I was only earning three pounds and fifteen shillings a week.

A Mr Gomm came into the shop one day and invited Bill and I to have a day's fishing on his private lake at West Wycombe in Buckinghamshire. Mr Gomm was the boss of 'G' Plan furniture, who had a factory on the North Circular Road, which I passed many times on the way to and from Walthamstow. By coincidence, a good friend and neighbour of ours, Paul Meadows, knew Mr Gomm well. During the War Paul had been a technician at de Havilland Aircraft in Hatfield, where they were building the Mosquito, a very successful all wood fighter/bomber. Apparently Mr Gomm had supplied many of the wooden components. It's a small world!

Anyway, we met Mr Gomm at the lake and were told that it was heavily stocked with rainbows in the 2–3 pound bracket and that there were also some very big fish there. He had caught one the previous year weighing 9½ pounds so they would be 10 pounds plus by now. The water was both deep and clear with a few scattered weed beds. We didn't see a fish move all day, nor did we see a single rise. I eventually caught a 3 pound rainbow by casting under an overhanging willow tree. In the evening Mr Gomm came down and we fished the outfall with the nymph. I did not have any so simulated one by cutting off the wings of a Greenwells Glory Yellowtag, which worked well and I soon had another 3-pounder.

Later I moved back to the lake and cast to a small dimpling rise. This can be caused by a small fish rising to the fly or a large fish swirling beneath the surface. Mr Gomm had advised us to use gut casts as the fish took so hard that they would snap a nylon one every time; then nylon was not as strong as it is now. This proved to be very true. Anyway, on my very first cast I had a take and before I could even get the rod up to what I could call a fighting position the fish had taken off up the centre of the lake and most of my line had gone with it! Needless to say, all went slack and I wound in to find that not only the fly, but also half the cast was missing. That fish was definitely one of the 'biggies' and I hate to think what it might have weighed.

Incidentally, Sir Henry Dashwood owned the famous mansion and park. The whole place had a notorious history, as it had been site of the eighteenth century

Hellfire Club founded by his ancestor Sir Francis Dashwood. This infamous Club was the venue for politicians and gentlemen to meet for wine, women and song. However we were only there for the fishing!

The City branch of Hardy Brothers closed down, owing to lack of business, so I was moved to the Pall Mall branch and Tom Parry was retired. After a few weeks in Pall Mall I was 'head hunted' by Ogden Smiths, whose main branch was just round the corner in St James. My decision to move was a big mistake as I just could not get on with any of the staff. Fortunately, it was not long before I got a job with Halliday's, a gun and tackle shop in Cannon Street in the City. The tackle side of the business was virtually non-existent until I arrived. I introduced fresh bait and, as we were the only shop in the City selling it, we quickly became very popular.

Norman Williams, who I had first met at Hardy's, was an insurance assessor for all the big properties in the south of England and he was a very meticulous and careful man. His army days on bomb disposal helped a lot I fancy! He got us a few days fishing on Viscount Mountbatten's water on the River Test at Romsey, Hampshire. On arrival at the water we were met by the bailiff, Bill Geary, who directed us upstream to a bend in the river, half spanned by a wooden fishing platform. On the very first cast I caught a brown trout of about 1½ pounds and this on bread flake. I hastily despatched and laid it on the bank behind me. Carrying on fishing I heard a rustle and turning saw a large rat making off with my trout. I hastily retrieved it and put in my bag for safety.

We continued to catch good roach, which pleased Norman as he was a roach fisherman by nature. I soon got fed up with this and decided to rig up my spinning gear and try for one of the large pike which were supposed to be in the water. Just then a man came down the opposite bank, following a large float in the middle of the river, which was flowing fast like all chalk streams do. He was almost running to keep up with it—was this the true meaning of long trotting?

I was fishing a 3 inch green/yellow Hardy plug, and just below the bridge had a crashing 'take'. The fish took me downstream fast until I was opposite the lawn of Broadlands House when it finally showed, and of course it was a salmon, slightly reddish and halfway to becoming a kelt. I managed to land it by getting it into the net head first and dragging it up the bank. I reckon it was 30 pound plus; what would it have weighed if fresh run? Just then Bill Geary came down the bank and asked what I had done with the fish. I said I had returned it to the water. He replied, "That's a pity as they smoke perfectly well and it will only die anyway". So ended another good day.

Whilst still at Halliday's we had an enquiry from a tea planter in Sri Lanka (Ceylon as it was then) for a large bore rifle, capable of killing elephants. After much 'phoning around we traced a double .600 rifle at Le Personne in the Old

Salmon fishing on the River Test, Broadlands Water.

Bailey. They had taken it in part-exchange for a pair of Browning shotguns and could not get rid of it, so we bought it for a ridiculous price. It was a beautiful gun, hammerless with side lock, made by Rigby of London. I went up to the Old Bailey to collect it, but forgot to take any sort of gun cover. However, the gun had a sling so I slung it over my shoulder and started back to Cannon Street on foot. I thought it advisable not to get on the bus! I got as far as the Royal Exchange when I was held up by crowds lining the streets to see King Saud of Saudi Arabia pass on his way to lunch at the Guildhall with the Lord Mayor of London. I stood there with the gun over my shoulder next to a young policeman who only had eyes for the King's wives in the following coach. He kept saying "Cor, look at that!" and took no notice of me or the gun. Imagine that in this day and age!

My next job was to take the rifle to the west London shooting grounds to test it on a target. The chief instructor was an ex-RAF corporal who was instructing on clay bird shooting. I remembered him vaguely from my war days. I had taken five cartridges, which weighed me down as they were magnums about 6 inches long, and of course the bullet was over ½ inch in diameter. The target was 30 inches in diameter and surrounded by earth walls, not very wide. The target

42

marker was a very short man who did various small jobs around the grounds and rode around on a pony and trap. I got fixed up with a sandbag to act as a rest, shooting from the prone position as I was told anything else would blow me over. Sure enough, the first shot nearly spun me round. Bear in mind that I was shooting over one hundred yards and the marker insisted on being close to the target, which was a trifle worrying. I finally got four reasonable hits and said "Wouldn't it be simpler to push a pencil through?" On arrival back in the City they asked me how I'd got on so I replied, "One miss, two outers, one pony and one dwarf!" However, our customer was very pleased and collected the gun— paying us a hefty profit.

By this time, through Mr Burt, we were stocking Luxor reels—and very popular they proved. Ken Greenfield, the junior partner, and I rented the shooting on a farm in Essex paying on a monthly basis. In September we shot most of the partridges, in October most of the pheasants but after that we packed it up as there were only a few rabbits left. Not bad for twenty quid! The old man was talking of retiring so Ken and I went down to Salisbury to suss out suitable premises for a shop of our own, but to no avail. All the agents had to offer were properties owned by the diocese and the rents were exorbitant. However, Ken did manage to buy someone out and he started up his own successful gun business.

Early transport 1947.

Chapter Nine

1960–1962
A Shop of My Own

I HAD BOUGHT a small shop in East Molesey, about one hundred yards from the River Thames and just over the bridge from Hampton Court Palace. The first year was diabolical; we were nearly going bust on a monthly basis! This was not helped by the fact that the Thames froze over in January 1963 to a depth of about six to eight inches. They roasted an ox at Kingston in memory of the old days and the lads from Comerford's, a motorcycle dealer at Thames Ditton, raced their bikes up and down the frozen river.

However, we recovered and one day a very smart AA patrol man came into the shop. As he was a craftsman, he was employed in lining out AA boxes. His name was Ted Cheeseman, hereafter referred to as E.C. We took an instant liking to

The River Thames frozen at Hampton Court bridge. Winter 1963.

each other and I ended up offering him a job at about one bob a week more than he was being paid by the AA. He accepted and soon proved his worth as a craftsman; he was an excellent rod builder.

Things were still not good at the shop and I had to give up the car for travelling to and fro and instead bought a pushbike. As soon as I could, I upgraded to a 50 cc NSU moped, which I fell off at regular intervals. At that time I was more or less existing on repairing rods and making USA steel aerials into spinning rods. I used the top two sections of the 12 foot aerial and cut them back to 7 foot. I had them stove enamelled black and they were half decent, with an action more like a banana than anything else! The original 4 foot butt I turned into landing net handles complete with cord handle, which were very popular. It is worth noting that I at first paid ten shillings for the aerials and then discovered you could buy them wholesale from the Army surplus for a halfpenny each. I was buying in a minimum of one hundred lots, which improved my profits as I was selling the finished rods for around three pounds each.

One day a man came into the shop asking to hire half a dozen rods for a fishing scene in the film *Three Men in a Boat*, starring Jimmy Edwards. He was prepared to pay five pounds per day each. I hastily got together six second-hand rods. Luckily for me it rained for three days so there was no filming. They paid me for the full four days, very nice too. East Molesey had quite a few stage and screen people in the area. I think this dates back to the days of Fred Karno, the comedian and theatre impresario, who built a sort of mini palace on Taggs Island, just above Molesey Weir. This had a dance floor, a gaming room and was the haunt of ladies of the night. There was no bridge in the early days and you had to rely on boats to ferry you to and fro. It was said that they charged you five bob to row you over and five quid to row you back! I reckon many a good dinner jacket was ruined when patrons had to swim back, having run out of money one way or the other. It was a wonder no-one got swept over Molesey Weir, which was only a few yards below the island.

There was also The Thames Hotel on the banks of the river, which was owned by Gladys Hay, the sister of Will Hay the comedian. It was one of the favourite watering holes for many of the local traders. Opposite this was The Carnarvon Arms and we also had The Prince of Wales and The Albion near my shop. So we were hardly short of pubs.

On the opening day of the 1960 fishing season, June 16th, a television crew arrived at the shop and interviewed me, saying I would be on the 6 o'clock news. I was home in good time to see it and Gill and Sue could not understand how I could be in two places at once!

Shortly after this the comedian, Charlie Drake came into the shop and asked to be fitted up with some tackle. I sold him a basic outfit and that evening took him down to the river and more or less showed him how to use it. At that time he had a partner, Jack Edwards, and they were appearing in a childrens' show called *Mick and Montmorency*. Later Charlie went solo and appeared in numerous television shows and films. His famous catch-phrase was, "Hello my darlings". We became quite good friends and coincidentally, we shared the same birthday, 3 September 1924. He had a shoot in Hertfordshire, which I went to many times and got plenty of pheasants and one roe deer.

One Sunday we took Gill and Sue over to his house in Weybridge. One of his neighbours was Eric Sykes, the comedian, who was also fishing that afternoon; they spent their time hurling insults at each other. Charlie's neighbour on the other side was a television presenter and he told me that Charlie had mentioned my interest in motorbikes and that he had one he would like me to see. It was a 350 cc transverse twin Velocette, the last model they ever made. I was thrilled as I had owned several Velo's in my biking days. I took it for a short spin up and down the road and it was wonderful and very fast. On returning to the house the man said, "I could not help noticing what a nice little bottom you have when you got on the bike". Believe me, I arrived back on Charlie's side of the hedge a lot quicker than I left!

Charlie was interested in buying into the firm, but having met his agent in Leicester Square, an ex-Army colonel, we could not agree on the rod building side so it came to nothing. He then bought into a tackle shop in Wimbledon which also operated a couple of boats out of Littlehampton for sea fishing. As I was already doing their rod repairs and selling them new rods I was pleased but it did not last long and they went bust within the year. Charlie passed away in 2006 at the grand age of eight-two years.

About this time I discovered that the shallows below the Mill at Cobham were teeming with minnows, which make good live bait for perch, pike and even the occasional chub. I used to knock the bottom out of wine bottles, thus forming a cone and place a piece of fine mesh over the neck and we were ready to go, with a few bits of bread in the bottle to act as an attracter. The shallows were easily wadeable and you hardly got your arm wet placing the bottles. On a good morning they would fill up with minnows in about ten minutes. Many a time I had to break the bottle to get them out. A few unfortunate sticklebacks, small gudgeon, stone loach, and bull heads (Miller's Thumbs) got caught as well and I returned these to the river if I spotted them. I reckon I was catching up to 1,000 a week, which was very rewarding at a retail price of two pennies each.

One day I noticed some 'boils' on the surface downstream and realised they were fish taking the bread which had been washed out of the bottles. Next day I took a rod with me, and using a clear plastic bubble float half filled with water to add weight for casting and baiting with a bread flake, I soon caught several chub, the largest being over 4 pounds. I only did this once as it was too time consuming and I needed to be back at the shop by 7.30 am and ready to open.

By this time I was employing three people apart from E.C. They were John Carpenter, Bob Waterhouse and Keith Ridgers. I also had a couple of part-timers: Bill Gaudian, a good fisherman who helped me on Saturdays, and my Sunday morning man, dear old Jock Caul. Jock worked for the Civil Service at Hampton Court Palace and he had an infinite capacity for Scotch whisky! I am still very much in touch with E.C. and write regularly and Gill has recently contacted Keith Ridgers on the internet, so another face from the past has re-surfaced. He is still fishing the River Mole and sent me a picture of himself in our old workshop. He is wearing a pristine white overall so it must have been early in the week as he was mainly employed with sticking on the cork shrives for the rod handles prior to machining. We used 'Cascomite' a quick setting water glue and he got smothered in the stuff. After a few days he did not bother to hang his overall up, he just dropped it in the corner as it was like a suit of armour!

In 1959 we moved from New Malden to East Molesey and we bought the singer Petula Clark's house on Riverside Avenue. I never met her but dealt with her father, Les, and her sister. Now we were only a mile from the shop, which made life much easier. Our new house had a river frontage on the River Ember in which I fished for dace and roach. We had a pair of kingfishers nesting in the opposite bank and we often saw them diving for minnows and other small fish. There was a firm called Trianco some way upstream by Ember Court, the police sports ground. They were located on a small weir and come the Easter holiday washed their cyanide plating tanks out in the river, which killed all the fish and water life. I was surprised at what floated down—large fish of many species which I did not know even existed. Luckily the poison became diluted before entering the main river—the Thames. The kingfishers disappeared straight away, either through eating poisoned fish or by lack of food.

One day Jimmy Nervo of the Crazy Gang, who appeared on stage at the Victoria Palace came into the shop for minnows. He had a powerboat moored on Taggs Island and wanted to catch perch, which lived under the nearby boats. He also ordered a 4 foot, one-piece rod, which he could take below decks without having to dismantle it. I delivered it the following week and nearing the boat heard a lot of laughter. There was Jimmy and his stage partner Teddy Knox surrounded by four or five girls from the chorus and a multitude of bottles! One of the girls asked me how it was done. I presumed she meant the fishing so I got into the stern of the boat and flicked a minnow under the next boat and immediately caught a nice perch. Jimmy came up and said it was better than he'd ever done, but, "Some people could catch fish in a piss pot!"

47

That same year one of my older customers came into the shop bearing a 25 pound pike which he had caught on one of my minnows in the Queen Mary Reservoir. Who says you need big baits for big fish? The minnow was at least 2 inches long! As the pike was still very much alive we put it in one of the livebait tanks and 'phoned London Zoo to see if they were interested. They said they were and a suitably equipped van would collect it. When it arrived we found that their idea of suitable equipment was a 12 inch washing-up bowl! We hastily wrapped the fish up in wet hessian sacking and told them to get it back to Regent's Park as quickly as possible. We 'phoned again the next day to be told that it had survived and was in a tank in the aquarium next to Richard Walker's (then record) 44 pound carp, caught in Redmire Pool.

Weir Wood Reservoir in Sussex had just opened and was well stocked with brown trout, all of a reasonable size. I remember one evening fishing with E.C. when he hooked a really good fish for the water, over 2½ pounds. I then forgot the golden rule; let the fish come to the net, never the other way round. I made a swipe at it and promptly knocked it off the hook. Sorry E.C.—I still dream about it over fifty years later!

Edna and I had a couple of holidays with her brother John and his wife Olive. Firstly we went to Selsey where I caught a small bass—around 1½ pounds, fishing at dawn off Selsey Bill using freshwater spinning tackle. Edna cooked it for my breakfast, I like my fish fresh! The following year the four of us went to Mersea Island and whilst there contacted Bob Mussett, who was a night

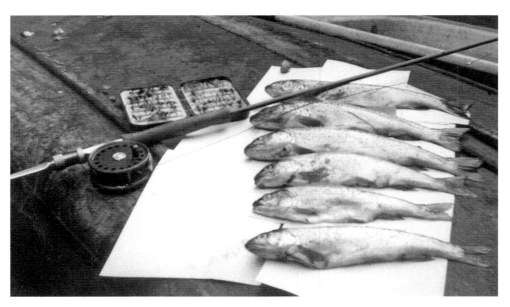

A fair bag of Trout. Weir Wood.

48

A few 'brownies', Weir Wood.

watchman in the City of London and came to Halliday's for his cartridges. He took John and me out in a boat one evening. A lone curlew, flying high, came over and John fired and brought it down. I don't know who was most surprised, John, me or the poor bloody curlew. It was probably the first and last shot he ever fired.

I went up to Mersea Island again and I lost a wader in the good old Essex mud trying to retrieve a merganser which I had shot. This made a trip to Colchester imperative to purchase a new pair of trousers and socks. I spent the rest of the day with one wader and one shoe, which curtailed my activities somewhat. We raided Bob Mussett's brother's oyster beds after dark and came back with a dozen natives each. Bob was like that, he always reckoned if he could not carry it he took his barrow and wheeled it!

All the lads at the shop had gone 'trout mad' by this time and our nearest venue was Shepperton Lakes, a complex of gravel pits which were still being worked. The rattle of the conveyor belts was a bit off-putting during working hours but it was well stocked with fish up to about 3 or 4 pounds. One Wednesday afternoon I was alone in the shop, E.C. and John Carpenter having gone to Shepperton. Trade was dead so after a while I thought, "Blow it", chucked the tackle in the car and went to join them. There was a heavy hatch of hawthorn flies. The nearest thing I had in my fly box were black gnats which worked well and I soon had several fish. There were dozens of water voles swimming about.

49

Yes, they were common in those days. I was using a three-fly cast and managed to straddle a vole. Hastily retrieving it I hooked it in the back by accident. It uttered a terrified squeak and made for a nearby island and disappeared. Just then E.C. came along and seeing my rod bent asked if I had a good fish on. I replied, "No, it's a vole that's gone down a hole." I applied pressure and got the lot back minus the vole, which I hoped was recovered after its fright.

Then there was Waggoner's Wells, twin lakes the other side of Hindhead in Surrey. I considered it to be understocked and there again a good fish was 3 or 4 pounds. E.C. tells me that the water keeper who collected the money used to engage him in conversation about his father's exploits in the First World War and was thus cutting into his fishing time. I never met him or else I could have bored him with my exploits in the Second World War, which would have resulted in no fishing at all! I do not recall ever meeting him or paying for that matter, probably due to the unearthly hours I kept in those days.

Then Sutton Bingham Reservoir on the Dorset-Somerset border opened and it was well stocked with good size fish. On the first opening day we arrived at the fishing hut at about 6 a.m., only to be told that it did not open until 8 a.m. There were four of us: E.C., John Carpenter, Jock Caul and myself. About 7.a.m. we were told we might as well start as we could only catch them once. I fished near the dam which must have been where they had released the stock fish as I caught my limit of eight fish in the first half an hour. I spent the rest of the day sitting on the bank, as it was before the days when you could buy another ticket. All the boys also did well and Jock managed to catch two fish at once and lose them both! The second day was as bad as the first was good. Despite walking round the Reservoir twice I failed to rise a single fish. The only one to score was John Carpenter who was fishing really deep with a worm fly; this was two Cock-y-bhondus tied together in tandem. Nothing like a worm really. Either he was really on the ball or too lazy to grease his line. Anyway it wasn't my style.

Whilst working in the City I met a dentist by the name of Frank Preston. He purchased a Hardy 8 cc de France dry fly rod designed by Pierre Creusevant, the well-known French casting champion. He extracted a few of my teeth and fitted a silver plate. I reckon what he charged me paid for his new rod. Anyway, we became good friends and I went for Sunday tea at his house in Hampstead. He was a member of a syndicate with water on the mid Itchen in Hampshire. He invited me down on several occasions. My lasting memory is of the huge dry fly box he carried. It must have had forty or fifty compartments, all full of flies he had tied himself.

The Itchen is a typical English chalk stream and in those days was inhabited by wild brown trout and grayling, not stocked fish. I soon found out that a rising trout made a neat circle on the surface, whereas a grayling made a long disturbance in the water. Whether this was due to their long dorsal fins or their hurry to reach the fly before anything else did is debatable. Anyway, the grayling were considered vermin to be taken out and killed. I did not mind catching them as they were easier to catch than trout and ate very well. A small side stream entered the stretch—this was the famous Barton Carrier, even Hardy's had named a trout reel after it—'The Barton Silent Trout Reel'. Silent, as the drag relied on leather pads instead of the normal ratchet, which was noisy; all done to preserve the peace of the place, which was fantastic.

I believe there is a motorway running close by these days which has ruined the whole peaceful feel of the place.

I was fishing downstream of Frank and there was a heavy hatch of blue-winged olives at the time and we both caught several good fish. The water was only about eighteen inches deep and when I glanced down to look at the top of my waders to make sure they were fully up I noticed a lot of red dots. I then realised they were hatching nymphs which had landed on me and were showing their little red tail lights!

Through Mr Burt I was now the sole agent for CP swing spoons made by Au Coin de Pêche in Paris. Very popular they were too. I advertised them in the *Fishing Gazette*, the angling paper in those days, and was soon sending them all over the country. One of my customers was Frankie Vaughan, the singer of 'Give me the Moonlight' fame. He was appearing in Brighton at the time and also fishing the Suffolk Ouse at Barcombe Mills for sea trout. I don't know if he ever caught any but he certainly purchased a lot of spoons. Maybe catching the bottom accounted for this. He always signed off his letters "with all my love"— strange people, these theatre folk! I did actually meet him once at Weir Wood Reservoir, which by that time had been infiltrated with coarse fish from the feeder stream and you were just as likely to catch a roach or a perch as a trout.

I too had a permit for Barcombe Mills and went down with John Stewart, whose father owned The Running Horses, a pub at the foot of Box Hill. It was a very good 'eaterie' and we patronised it regularly. On this occasion we were night fishing and it was the eve of my birthday—I forget which one. It had been raining hard all day and we found the river in full flood and over the banks. The weir pool was a seething cauldron and it was hard to find where the bank ended, so I stood well back, having no desire to fall into that lot. As it was almost pitch dark I used a bright yellow Pfluegar plug bait, thinking it would be more visible to the fish. You could forget the old advice for catching sea trout, which was 'spin by day and fly by night.' There was no way you could have used a fly rod in the prevailing conditions. On only my third cast I hooked a fish that took me all over the pool before I finally netted it. It proved to be a sea trout of 8¾ pounds and the best fish of any species I ever caught. It was close run by another sea

Gill with a 8¾lb sea trout at Barcombe Mills, 1956.

trout of 8 pounds which I caught on the River Stinchar on the west coast of Scotland, this time on the fly and by day—a complete reversal of the old advice.

There was an arboretum down in Surrey, I forget quite where, which had a lake with a punt which you could book for two people. There was no bank fishing and it was sparsely stocked but the fish were large. I had a day there with Jock Caul and did not see a single rise all day. On returning the punt to the boathouse I noticed a high wall adjacent. Looking down I saw a good fish slowly circling and feeding on nymphs of one sort or the other. As I still had my rod up and tackle up I hastily dropped a fly in front of it which it immediately took. After a short fight Jock netted it for me, it proved to be a brown of 2½ pounds. It did not stand much of a chance as I was standing directly above it and there was no way it could make a run. It occurred to me that it might be somebody's pet as it was so trusting and close to the bank. Never mind, it ate very well. So much for no bank fishing!

In the shop at that time we were making Spanish reed match rods, mainly 10–12 foot, two-pieces, with the odd three-piece. They were the very devil to make. Firstly, they would not go into the lathe, so the cork handles had to be finished by hand, firstly using a coarse file and then various grades of sandpaper. The top sections had to be doubly spliced, firstly with a short length of tonkin cane and then a split cane tip of say 3 foot or 3 foot 6 inches. Then all the knots had to be whipped over, and there were plenty on the Spanish reed. I could make maximum of two a week and that meant staying up until midnight whipping them and then being up at 6 a.m. to catch minnows. Anyway, we built quite a few and supplied the whole of the Molesey Angling Club as they were so popular.

Jock Caul with 2lb brown trout from Aboretum Fishery.

I had a customer and friend named Pete for whom I made an 8 foot fly rod. He also fished Barcombe Mills. He took me down one day on the back of his 500 cc International Norton, which he had modified by putting the power unit into the new Norton featherbed frame. He reckoned it made him 10 mph faster round the bends. I never doubted it! The rods which were slung over my shoulder bent at an angle of 60 degrees through sheer wind pressure.

By this time Chew Valley had opened and was heavily stocked with good sized fish. On numerous visits I don't think I caught one under 2 pounds. The same Pete was a regular visitor to Chew and he told me that if I arrived before dawn I should go to Nunnery Point where I would hear the fish sloshing about. They were after roach fry which also abounded. Pete said, "Don't bother to cast to them as you can't see anyway, just cast out and they will find it". It turned out to be true and I had a few nice fish. I was using a size 8 Alexander, a peacock green wing fly with silver body and red tail.

I was at the Angling Show at the Royal Horticultural Hall, at which we exhibited. There was a large casting pool to show off various rods and reels. It was about twelve inches deep. Bernard Cribbins, the well-known actor and a customer of mine, came to my stall and asked to borrow a pair of waders.

2nd London trade show. 1960.

Without thinking I gave him a pair with metal studs on the soles; he then grabbed one of the publicity 'dolly birds' and careered up and down the pool. Needless to say, he punctured the polythene liner and from having twelve inches of water in the pool we had about two inches all over the floor. Guess who got the blame for that!

I went for a drink at the bar and stood next to Tom Ivens, who was an ex-Lieutenant Commander in the Navy and wrote the original book *Still Water Fly Fishing*. I ordered a pink gin and he turned to me and asked if I had been in the Navy too. I replied, "No the RAF, I just happen to like pink gin!" His book was most interesting—centred on the rod he used, a 10 foot, two-piece called the Iron Murderer. He had three flies which he relied on and tied himself—the Alexander, the Black and Peacock Spider and the 'Pretty Pretty', a muddle of various blues. He also devoted a chapter to the 'Double Haul' method of casting for distance. This meant hauling on the line at the end of the cast, thus accelerating its progress through the air.

Mr Burt took us to Paris to meet our suppliers, Jacques Michel of Pezon et Michel, suppliers of Luxor reels and a whole range of split cane rods. They were the 'Hardy's' of France. Our hosts took us out for an evening meal at 'Jour et Nuit', a very posh restaurant on the Champs d'Elysees. The main dish was the *fruites de mer*, which was a huge platter with a lobster each surrounded by jumbo prawns, oysters, clams, and other seafood. It must have cost a fortune even in those far off days. We also had lunch with the directors of Au Coin de Pêche, makers of the CP spoon, for which I was the British agent. Then we met with the manufacturers of Lerc glass fibre blanks to whom we gave a nice order. As it was Mr Burt's turn to host a meal, he took us to a small restaurant opposite Notre Dame Cathedral for a bowl of fish stew. I can't spell the French name, but it's very famous. It was excellent, even though I was sick in the middle of the night!

In the meantime E.C. had acquired a Tom Ivens Iron Murderer. I am not sure if he bought it or built it himself; if the latter, I am not sure where he got the split cane from, or who made it. It was a brute of a rod, more likely to murder you instead of the fish, as E.C. found out after a long day at Waggoner's Wells when he came back with a severe case of tennis elbow.

I was still going to Enton Lakes fairly regularly and on one hot day with hardly a ripple on the water there were no signs of any fish. All the punts were out so I had to fish from the bank. Come evening the whole surface of the upper lake erupted with rising fish, but the punts were still not catching. I noticed that silver sedges were hatching. The nearest thing I had in my fly box was a Partridge and Silver which I tied on and soon had my limit, which I believe was four fish in those days.

John Birth and I decided to have a day on the bridge pool on the River Avon at Christchurch. This was bookable in advance and was from a punt for two people. It was secured to both banks by a rope and you could pull it to and fro to obtain the best position. Although tidal, the water remained fresh as an incoming tide merely pushed the water up. We had special permission to fish on after dark from the bank using fly only. We started off by spinning from the bank. I was using a 1½" Rublex diving plug and soon had several nice sea trout. The water keeper came along and said "You'll soon outstay your welcome doing that, you've paid for the punt, so get in it". What a rude man!

Anyway, we went afloat and as usual the pool was full of dace all about 10 inches long. Every trot down produced a fish. Then a broad northern accent bellowed out, "Ee, lad's dropped t'glasses". I looked up and saw a huge man and an owl-faced kid staring down at the water. He then said, "Can'st get 'em?" I still had my waders on from the morning's efforts but they were rolled down. I got out of the boat and filled my right one with cold water—was I pleased! I started searching about with my hands when he said, "It's an 'orn rimmed pair". By this time I was fed up and shouted back "How many bloody pairs are down here?" I did find them and he said "Tie 'em to top of t'rod and pass 'em up to me". I thought, yes, and risk you breaking off the top 6 inches of my rod. No thank you. I told him to get onto the bank and I would throw them to him, which I did and he departed without a word of thanks.

We continued catching dace until I finally managed to get through them and had a nice sea trout. I immediately changed to a ½ ounce Arlesey Bomb instead of float tackle and from then on was catching sea trout regularly. This coincided with a high tide which brought a good run of fresh fish. At one time I was catching a fish a cast—all between 1 and 2 pounds. John was slower than I was in changing his tackle and being an all out fly fisherman was not quite with 'touch ledgering'. We caught between fifty and sixty fish between us, of which I'm afraid to say, I caught the bulk. Then the Bridge Hotel lowered lunch to us from the parapet and I was amazed to see half a lobster each, half a bottle of champagne and strawberries and cream. I wondered who was going to pay for this little lot, but luckily sold half of my catch back to the hotel for one pound each, thus making twenty pounds, which paid for the permits, lunch and even my petrol.

So we went ashore for the late evening session using fly only. I started by using a 1½ inch tube fly of my own tying with green peacock head and silver body and size 8 Mustad Treble. I caught a couple of small fish and then kept fouling the bottom as the tide was going out. I changed the hook to a size 10 Pezon et Michel fine wire treble, which proved to be a fatal mistake. I then got a strong 'take'. At first I thought it was a salmon and then remembered that salmon do

Stag hunt 3. Devon 1961.

told me it was unnecessary as she had found a bottle of red in the cocktail cabinet. This proved to be a bottle of Croft's '45 vintage port. I had bought a bottle the previous Christmas and it was so good that I went out and bought another bottle for the next year's celebrations. I believe they cost me forty-five shillings each. There was an off-licence near where we are living now which specialised in vintage wines and sure enough at the top of their list of ports was Crofts '45, costing several hundreds of pounds. It was better than I thought! There was so much of the hare and port that I 'phoned Bob Waterhouse to come and share it with us. He did so and we all finished up slightly pissed.

Mr Burt had lost his first wife through cancer and had remarried. He was a small man, about 5 foot 5 inches and his new wife was an Amazon, at least 5 foot 11 inches. He asked me to give her some fly fishing instruction. I took her to the boating pool at the end of the Leg of Mutton Pond in Bushy Park. She was so tall I could barely reach her wrist to guide her through the various movements necessary to cast a fly. Fortunately, there were no spectators as we must have made a pretty sight. As I was halfway up her back we could have been done for indecent behaviour!

The very first sporting goods and fishing tackle show took place in London and I shared a room with Henry Aitken. We presented the Superflex range of rods, which were well displayed on a stand made by E.C. It was there that I first met Ken Smith who was to become a good friend later on. He had just won the 1960 national angling match, fished on the River Yare in Norfolk. I believe it was a record catch, 60 pounds of bream. We presented him with the best rod in our range and the other exhibitors did the same. With all these rods and his prize money from the match he opened a tackle shop in Norwich, which was quite a jump up from working in a shoe factory and selling day-old chicks at the weekend. There's more about Ken Smith later, after we moved to Norfolk.

I made a couple of trips to the Border Esk, staying at the Ashley Bank Hotel in Langholm, a hostelry we were to use many times in the future. The first trip was with Paddy Ward, a senior pilot with BOAC. We fished a lower stretch courtesy of John Birth whose boss at Enton Lakes had a long lease on it. Unfortunately, the river was full of kelts from last autumn's run and it was so cold that the first ten yards or so of the river was frozen over. It was almost a fish

1st London trade show. 1959.

a cast and it was fun sliding them over the ice. Of course, there was no fight in them. Paddy did at last manage to catch a 'baggot', a female kelt, which put up a good fight and was at least edible.

I had another trip with Paddy, this time to the far north west of Scotland. We stayed at Loch Inver, at a hotel owned by an old casting friend, whose name escapes me. Once again we were too early and although the salmon were trying to run they could only get as far as the sea pool, owing to lack of water in the river. They would not take in salt water. At low tide you could see them lying on their sides like so many silver dustbin lids. Very frustrating! However, we had a good time with the trout in the River Inver and also the numerous hill lochs.

There were further trips to Langholm. Once I went with John Birth and although the salmon were present we blanked once more but did manage some decent sea trout fishing at night. On another trip, this time at night after heavy rain, there was a small spate which lifted the salmon upstream. They went straight through our stretch and up to the spawning grounds in the headwaters. I tried every pool and never saw a single one. On our last night I went for sea trout at Cannonby, the limit of our water, and fished the long pool for sea trout. It was about three hundred yards long, mainly a sand bank. By the time I got there, there were about ten other anglers already in position. I managed to get in about halfway down the pool and soon had several fish in the 2 to 3 pound bracket. I then packed it in and saw that the other anglers had formed a queue behind me to take up my position and ask me what fly I was using.

Meanwhile, back at the shop we were making 11 foot, three-piece Avon rods. These had whole Tonkin cane butts and split cane middle and top sections. The prototype had a 9/16 inch tensile alloy butt, which made it much lighter. Unfortunately, I sold this before finding I could not get any more alloy for the butt sections. I had a penchant for selling my own rods. The customers thought it would make them a better angler. Some hopes!

Then, I had a surprise when a Captain Razywski came into the shop. He was a Polish gentleman who had been a good customer when I was with Hardy's in the City. Despite their huge range of rods he would always insist on a rod being specially made for him with slight alterations from standard. He probably thought he was getting a better rod this way and was probably right. I can see him now, he would inspect it for straightness and stand back and utter the one word 'beauty'. I do not think he ever fished with them, merely kept them to admire. I duly made him a 'special' fly rod and took him to Weir Wood to teach him to fly cast and hopefully catch some trout, which unfortunately he failed to do. He was a Captain in the Polish Army and edited the Polish free newspaper in London. He had not seen his wife and children since the Germans invaded

Poland, thus starting the Second World War. He told me later that they all became victims of one of the Nazi death camps in the Holocaust.

At this time the shop was doing really well, particularly in the bait section. Apart from the ever-popular maggots and minnows we were selling 2,000 marsh worms a week, obtained from a sewage farm in Sutton. We also sold a hundredweight of hemp a week, the bait par excellence for roach on the Thames. We sold the hemp seed ready boiled, just enough to split open, allowing the sprout to appear and allow the bend of the hook to push in. Each week we also sold a hundredweight of 'pinhead' crampon, which was normally used by butchers as sausage filler, but made an excellent ground bait. In those days the crampon was mixed in the ratio of 5% to 95% pork for sausages. Today that ratio has been reversed, 95% filler and 5% pork, if you are lucky!

Chapter Ten

1962–1965
A Big Mistake

THEN I made the biggest mistake of my life. Paddy Ward suggested to me that I move into larger premises. This I duly did, to a shop across the road. It was at least four times as big as the existing one, plus a large back room and spacious cellar. This meant changing my bank, which caused a row between the manager and me. My new bank owned the shop, which adjoined it, and also the two upper floors, one occupied by a solicitor and the other by a firm of accountants. Not a good set up! The problem was stocking the new shop. Paddy put up £1,000 and I got some support from my trust fund and the bank also promised to help me. So we were set to go.

The second shop. Bridge Street, Molesey, 1963.

We turned the old shop into a pet food shop in partnership with John Hines, an old fishing mate. Our wives, Edna and Shirley-Anne, staffed it and John and I delivered pigeon food once a week. This did not last long and I sold the shop to an antique dealer who had been my next door neighbour. I rejected an offer from a firm of bookmakers despite numerous threats of damage to my health!

Things went well at first in the new premises, but then went slowly downhill. This was not helped by a new shop opening on the arcade right opposite the railway station. With anglers pouring off the trains, this is where the bulk of my trade had been coming from. I had invested the cash from the sale of the small shop in the business so was really out on a limb. My last customers of note were Michael Bentine of *The Goon Show* and Mick Jagger who came in occasionally.

There is an interesting interlude concerning Thames trout. A small band of dedicated men would gather on the gantry over the main flow of Molesey Weir and spin for trout with a dead bleak mounted on a spinning tackle. After about an hour adjusting the tackle so it spun true they carried on for some hours. I never heard of a fish being caught. However, one Sunday a lad came into the shop and bought some maggots and went down to the Thames and fished just below Hampton Court Bridge. Half an hour later he was back asking if I had a camera as he had caught a large fish and would like a photo of it. It proved to be a 4 pound Thames trout.

On another occasion, E.C. and I were fishing the River Mole behind Paynes Hill Lake. E.C. was fishing plug bait and, I believe, caught a small pike, while I opted for a small weir halfway up the stretch. At first I did not get a single bite and then remembered what I had learned on Molesey Weir. That is, flicking the bare hook onto the apron and picking up a small piece of blanket weed. This was the bait and was deadly. The fish take it and crush it, releasing all the small water life it contains. I soon had several good roach.

4lb Thames Trout, Molesey.

Molesey Weir.

I enjoyed a very good day on the Army Officer's water on the Upper Avon—
Nether Avon, to be exact. This was by courtesy of an old King's friend, Peter
Newmarch, an ex-Army captain. I was met by the bailiff, Frank Sawyer, who was
responsible for the Sawyer Nymph. He gave me some to try and all they
consisted of was a few turns of copper wire on the hook shank and a bit of
ginger hackle. I doubted if they would work as the river was running down after
a spate and was full of bits of rubbish floating down, but I was proved wrong.
Frank would say "There's a feeding fish ten yards upstream by that hassock on
the opposite bank". I could cast fairly well in those days and so caught it. I was
puzzled how he could see the fish but later realised that the inside of a trout's
mouth is white and he could spot the jaws opening. What eyesight! He finally had
a rod named after him, the Sawyer Nymph rod made by Pezon et Michel in Paris.
I sold quite a few.

About this time I had taken on a partner in the rod building side of the
business and the first thing he did was sever our links with Henry Aiken and
Superflex rods. He decided we would only market our own rods, which meant a
long uphill battle if we got the orders and also a large investment in raw
materials. I could foresee trouble coming and had already made arrangements to
make rods for the East Anglian Rod Company based in Norfolk. Then the
crunch came and I was out. In addition to the Purdey gun, I also left behind all
my personal tackle and tournament gear. On 'phoning the shop I was told I

71

would have to buy it like everyone else. I don't particularly blame E.C. for this as he was obeying orders from above but I was blowed if I would pay for my own tackle so I let it go. I often wonder what happened to my other Browning 2-shot automatic personal gun, which finished up broken under the wheels of a tractor at the Guildford Clay Pigeon Club at Clandon, Surrey. An insurance job one would think!

I had been quite keen on tournament casting and really cleaned up in the first year, winning three events as an amateur. The next year I only won the ⅝th accuracy although I believe E.C. won the ⅜th distance. The following year I cast in the world championships in Rotterdam to no avail.

Luckily, I had my two split cane fly rods and my MK IV Pentax SLR camera at home. I sold the latter back to David Ross who had the local photographic shop in Molesey and bought a very second-hand Hillman Husky for forty-five pounds, as I had also lost my Volvo estate. It stood me in good stead and got me to Norfolk and back many times. I completed my time in Molesey working for Pegley-Davies in Hersham. I was making ferruless Lerc rods and doing all their Penn reel repairs.

About this time we purchased a 10 foot Mirror dinghy from a man who lived just upstream from us on the River Ember. At first we kept it moored at the bottom of our garden and then moved it to Martins boathouse on the River Thames near the shop and just above Hampton Court Bridge. This enabled us to rent it out for fishing and it soon paid for itself. I never did pick up the sails, mast and all the other gear as we only wanted it for fishing, not sailing. It was eventually sold and replaced with a 14 foot clinker-built Dory made in the Aran Islands. It was really too long and difficult to turn round in the narrow River Ember. What happened to it I do not know as at the time I was busy setting up a rod business in Norfolk and training up new and completely inexperienced staff. I was also looking for a place to live as I was in temporary digs. Anyway, it was my own property having been paid for from my personal account. It was moored in the usual place at the bottom of the garden when it went missing. The 'Molesey Mafia' at work again no doubt!

Chapter Eleven

1966–1976
Norfolk

I HAD BY this time joined up with the East Anglian Rod Company as a rod builder and moved up to Norfolk. We were first based in Colton in an old disused farmhouse, having first got the squatters out! After much cleaning up and making a room suitable for varnishing we were ready to go, having purchased my old rod lathe and cork dust extractor unit from my old firm. I was pleasantly surprised to find that the locals took to the various new jobs like ducks to water. I was in digs in a farm labourer's cottage and my landlady, her neighbour and daughter soon picked up the skills of whipping (attaching the rings to the rod with fine silk with no gaps or overlaps). I also had a very good girl varnishing the rods.

Anyway, we sold No 1 Riverside Avenue in Molesey in 1966 and purchased Southfields, a large country house in Wicklewood free standing in over an acre of ground. It had several outbuildings, two of which were 'clay lump', fashioned from a mixture of straw and clay. Surprisingly they were very durable. The builders had obtained the clay from just inside the front gates, leaving a hole which quickly filled with water so I was able to keep ducks as well. The property also contained two large chicken sheds, both about 100 feet by 30 feet. I had one fitted with a cement floor and an outside shed for the dust extractor and then moved the whole rod building business from Colton to my home. I changed my staff and found the local girls even better than those at Colton, at finishing rods that is! Anyway, two girls would whip fifty rods per week each, which was about our normal output. That, and a girl varnishing the rods on the premises, was about it. John Carpenter, my ex-employee also whipped the rods up for me and continued to do so even though I was making them in Norfolk. I used to meet him halfway in Newmarket to exchange rods and cash.

I set up another source of income in the other chicken shed. Mrs Woodcock, the previous owner of Southfields, had left me a follow-on brooder plus all the feeders and equipment. I bought one hundred day-old white eggers and started them off before moving them to the vacant shed where they soon produced high yields of large eggs. I had no trouble selling them as they were so good and much better than the battery variety.

I had already made contact with Ken Smith who had a shop in Norwich and I made quite a few rods for him. Together we designed the 'Ken Smith' quiver tip rod for East Anglian and sold quite a few. It was made from the top two sections of a Lerc 12 foot match blank with the top cut off and a finely tapered solid glass tip spliced in. It proved to be a deadly weapon and won many matches. Ken had rented a piece of water at Lenwade and stocked it with trout. It was good fishing and on a cold morning in March I caught the all time record, a fish just under 3 pounds. This was quite a battle as the line froze in the rings making it impossible for me to give or take line. I finally managed to make it succumb and 'beached' it by walking backwards up the bank.

Sue, our youngest daughter, was showing a great interest in horses. It is a hobby she has retained until this day. She started going with her friend, Dawn, to Mr Jack Juby's stables in Morley. Jack was a great character and well known in shire (heavy horse) circles for specialising in Percherons. He was awarded the MBE in 2002 in recognition of his services to the industry and his work brought him into contact with many Royals, including the Queen, Prince Philip and

My record trout. Ken Smith's water at Lenwade.

Prince Charles. We bought Sue her first pony, a little grey named Major and stabled him in one of the clay lump buildings.

The Dunston Harriers, who hunted the hare on horseback instead of the more usual way of on foot, had a meet at The Cherry Tree, our local pub. While the hunt was enjoying the traditional 'stirrup cup' at the pub, a hare appeared running fast across the field at the back of our house. It was hotly chased by the hounds, then Sue on Major and, rather belatedly, the rest of the hunt!

One day a rep arrived selling rod blanks, the basic tapered tube from which we made the rods. He took me out to lunch at a local hostelry and I gave him a small order. The next week he came back with the blanks and as we were short of time, we had lunch in the house. He then noticed a photo on the wall of 218 Squadron air crew and said, "I was with that lot!" Of course he was Roland Bishop, my old mate from 218 and our motorcycling days. He was to play a large part in my life later on.

Now, a few words concerning rods and lines. If I had my time again I would still go for an 8 foot 9 inch two-piece parabolic action split cane fly rod for trout and sea trout. For all general coarse fishing, I would use an 11 foot, three-piece Avon style rod with split cane middle and top and whole Tonkin butt.

To manufacture the fly rod, I would obtain some first class split cane, preferably from Bob Southwell of Croydon. Then I would form an 8 inch cork handle above a small screw grip reel fitting. The corks would be shaped to fit the hand, ending with a reversed mushroom at the top end to provide a pressure point for the thumb when making the forward cast. I would then fit a quality 'splint end' reinforced ferrule to join the two sections together. The same process applied to the 11 foot Avon rod except we fitted a 28 inch cork handle on the butt, turned down to 1 inch parallel to take 1 inch sliding winch fittings which were fully adjustable for positioning of the reel, again fitting splint end ferrules. The fly rod had shake intermediate rings with agate butt and tip and the Avon rod had low bells life intermediates with stand-off agate butt and tip.

Regarding ferrules, the reinforcement was a small band at the top of the female ferrule to stop it belling out with use. The splint end meant that the end of the ferrule that went first on the rod was tapered down very finely and then cross cut in three places thus forming a splint for each of the hexagonal faces of the split cane. It was then whipped down with silk. Incidentally, Ron Chapman, maker of the famous '500' rod (which was amazingly cheap—we sold dozens) came up with the idea of a five-sided split cane fly rod instead of the normal hexagon. I imagine this presented all sorts of manufacturing problems. I never tried one but heard they were very good.

On a trip to the Midlands to attend a tackle show I met a well-known contributor to a national weekly paper. As he lived more or less in the centre of the tackle trade I asked where I could get ferrules as I was thinking of building a few rods again. All I got was a blank look and "What's a ferrule?" in reply!

The other thing to bear in mind is that we got ferrules from the manufacturers in the untreated brass state and they had to be bronzed before fitting. As we used the 'cold' method this involved the use of cyanide, not the best of things to have lying around. As things improved on the rod building side we took to using nickel silver ferrules by Pezon et Michel of Paris. They had everything, including reinforcements and splint ends and they even bronzed them for you. They were expensive, but well worth it. This is all in the past as I hear bored corks are now one pound each instead of the halfpenny we used to pay—how many did I throw away in the past? The cheapest ferrule, just plain, no reinforcement or splint end, is now ten pounds. It's enough to put anyone off rod building for life.

As far as fly lines are concerned, we started off with silk double taper lines. There were three of note: the Corona Superba (the best), the Corona and the Kingfisher. The same firm made them all but the latter was the only one available to the trade in general. Then an American by the name of Marvin K. Hedge came up with the idea of a forward taper which would cast thirty yards, a previously unheard of distance. Ogden Smiths marketed this; I tried one and didn't like it!

The company Scientific Anglers, also American, came up with the first 'Aircel'. This was a plastic line built up in tapers over a parallel nylon core. The first ones were white and very prone to cracking particularly if bunched up in the hand when retrieving line. Scientific Anglers overcame this but not before I had replaced quite a few with no remuneration. They went on to produce a whole range of lines in all weights and colours but I thought that any line cast a shadow on the water. They produced floating, sinking, fast sinking and sink tip in all weights and colours. I imagine the high visibility ones like yellow and orange gave the angler an indication of where his fly was—something he should have known in the first place.

It is not uncommon these days for anglers fishing the big boat matches to take five or more spare reels with them with varying lines plus three or four rods to cover every eventuality. I'd like to see them do this from the shore. No, give me a silk D tapered line No 4 old number which would balance the 8 foot 9 inch parabolic rod perfectly. If you wanted it to float you greased it, if you wanted it to sink you didn't. Easy, wasn't it!

Ken Smith got an order for a special beach casting rod, which I duly made and presented to a Mr Jarvis. He owned about three-quarters of a mile of the River Wensum and, in return, gave me sole permission to fish there. He was a cucumber grower by trade and had a series of greenhouses along the banks of the river. He used a method I had never seen before; bales of straw with two

76

hollows scooped out were soaked in water and filled with compost for the plants. It was so successful he employed a team of girls, who literally ran from one greenhouse to the next in the gathering season as the cucumbers were so quick growing. He also grew tomatoes using the same method and was proud of the fact that you could grow both in the same greenhouse.

Now to the fishing—which was superb. The river, in those days was gin clear and fast flowing like a Hampshire chalk stream. It was full of quality roach, dace and the occasional wild brown trout, which could be caught on the fly. I found out that by holding back on the float, which in turn caused the bait to lift in the water, and then releasing it at the end of the swim you could catch really good grayling in the 2 pound class. They were obviously too shy to join in the general melee after our loose feed. I think it was the best coarse fishing I ever enjoyed. There was an eddy on a bend at the lower end of the stretch, which held several pike. I had one of about 5 pounds on a live dace that I had caught earlier. As the water was so clean, I kept it and Edna cooked it. Very good it was too, apart from the bones. Strangely, Mr Jarvis never fished the river as he was an out and out beach man.

I had joined the Wymondham and District Angling Club and in the first year fished all the big 'open' matches. These were mainly fished on local rivers such as the Witham, Welland Ten Mile Bank and the Relief Channel, which were all dead straight and featureless. You either drew a peg on a shoal of fish or you did not. In my case it was always 'not'! That was until the Waveney 'open' fished in the Beccles area. We had that week designed and built an 8 foot swing tip rod. On arrival at my peg it looked ideal for swing tipping and I caught right from the start finishing up with 18 pounds, including two 4 pound bream and won the match plus one hundred pounds, which was a lot of money in those days. My upstream neighbour was a supposed crack Midland angler; he didn't catch a thing and at the final whistle threw his rod down and jumped on it. I hope he was sponsored! On the coach back to headquarters in Beccles he kept on talking about local knowledge, but I had never even seen the river before. It turned out he was a canal fisherman and used to catching fish in the 2–3 inch range.

I went on a pike fishing trip to Ranworth Inner Broad, which was only opened for a short period. It was dead bait fishing from a boat, casting just short of the reed beds. Several good fish were caught although I only had one run and I missed it!

I remember Jim Knights, who much later was to become Jean Smith's second husband after Ken died. On returning to the main broad I put my bait just off the landing stage as there were several dogs about and I did not particularly wish to hook one. I then went to the pub with for a pint with Jim when someone came in to say my rod was being carried away. I rushed and caught it just in time and found I had hooked a 20 pound pike—the only one I ever caught!

I had, by this time, packed in making rods for a living after a row with my boss at the East Anglian Rod Company. This was in 1969 and after a short spell of inactivity, I landed a job at Lotus Cars through Freddie Bushell. Freddie was the father of Erica who was a great friend of my daughter, Sue. He was a very nice man and it was a great pity he, as chief accountant, had to be the fall guy in the DeLorean affair in 1982. They were an American outfit and they went bust after producing just a handful of cars. By all accounts, Lotus, who were responsible for the stainless steel and fibreglass bodies had borrowed heavily from the British Government and lost the lot. DeLorean got away with it but poor Freddie did several years in prison in Northern Ireland where the car was made.

At first I was on the Lotus Europa assembly line, sticking bits on cars. This was very boring, so at the first opportunity I got a transfer to the fibreglass shop. Here I started in Resinject and progressed to Techocraft, and then to the Mystère luxury cabin cruiser. Whilst working there I learned the art of fibreglass laminating, a skill which was to stand me in good stead in later days in Ireland.

Ken Smith sold his house in Norwich and bought a piece of land at Tasburgh containing two lakes. He and Jean, his wife lived in a caravan on site until their bungalow was built. He had a third lake made by excavating on the banks of the River Tas. It was very much a 'meat for manners' job as the contractors got the gravel and Ken got his lake. He called it Broadwing after the sedge fly, which was there in abundance. All three lakes were stocked with trout, both brown and rainbow. To attract customers he ran a series of introductory fishing lessons on a Saturday. He would give a general talk, then his youngest son, Robin, would talk about pond life and show the various nymphs that he had netted from the lakes and their imitations, which they also sold. Then it was my turn to demonstrate casting and show them the mechanics, both as a group and individually. Most of our customers had brought with them a rod of some sort, usually with a line that did not match. It was strange moving down the line of complete beginners with all their different actions. One man would have a brand new graphite rod as stiff as a broomstick and the next an ancient greenheart which cast like a piece of wet string!

I had a letter from a George Cole, the managing director of a fibreglass firm in Southern Ireland, to go over and investigate the possibility making a range of fishing rods. Roland Bishop was already there making the blanks as he did in England. They flew me to and fro in their private Cessna, piloted by Peter Horne who had been George's instructor at Oxford Flying School before joining the firm. They did not have any equipment suited for rod making, so after making a couple of personal rods for George, I returned home to Lotus Cars and Ken Smith.

I continued to give instruction at Ken's lakes, this time to individuals. I could earn more on a Saturday afternoon and a couple of evening sessions than I could from a whole week's work at Lotus. However, Ken had a disaster. After a heavy rainstorm, Broadwing (being the lowest of the lakes) overflowed into the adjacent River Tas, taking most of the trout with it. They finished up below the road bridge outside Ken's property. Of course this was open water, available for anyone to fish. The bridge was soon lined with small boys catching trout up to 2 pounds in weight on a worm. Very galling I should think!

Unfortunately Ken died a few years later while we were living in Ireland and his wife, Jean, turned the complex into a carp and general coarse fish fishery before selling up and moving out.

E.C. organised a small tackle show and casting competition in Leatherhead and I took a few of our rods down and duly entered the casting. I came away with three cups—I forget for which events, but I certainly showed them how to do it.

Through a local landlord I obtained sole permission to fish the Cheshire Homes Lake. Early morning sessions produced plenty of small roach and rudd and some good-sized crucian carp up to 2 pounds in weight. These were to be the first and last I ever caught. There were a lot of Muscovy ducks on the lake and their eggs were very good; I took many home with me. After a while the lake was taken over by Eastern Counties Newspapers' Angling Club and so that was the end of that for me.

In the meantime Sue had met Ernie, a relationship that produced Marc, our only and dearly beloved grandson. Edna and I were the only ones present at his birth in the early hours of the February 4th 1973. Marc lived with us for three years, with Edna looking after him while Sue worked as a hairdresser. Sue and Ernie married and moved to a house in Spooner Row. They had our grand-daughter Melanie in 1983.

A few years later I had a further letter from George Cole, offering me a job as rod maker for Shannon Vale Plastics, in Clonakilty, County Cork. This time I accepted his offer and flew out to Ireland again, this time by Aer Lingus, an airline we were to use many times in the future.

Chapter Twelve

1976–1988
Ireland

W E SOLD Southfields and Edna and I moved out to Ireland. We were based in Clonakilty, a small coastal town in County Cork in the south-west. After a few weeks living in Roland Bishop's caravan in the grounds of his bungalow, I found a three-storey town house in the centre of Clon, which I rented and later purchased. I had a small disused school for a workshop about two hundred yards from my house. Soon I had four or five local girls whipping rods and another two varnishing. Meanwhile, I was in the front room doing all the construction work. I employed James O'Donohue, who was to become a firm friend and companion on many fishing expeditions. We had a contract with Woolworth's and made them hundreds of rods.

The fishing was quite good locally as we had the Brandon and Argideen rivers and the little local River Feal which flowed through Clonakilty, about twenty yards from our house. The wildlife was fantastic. Whilst walking Rip, our Jack Russell terrier, one evening along the banks of the Feal I noticed a 'boil' on the surface and thought it was one of the large mullet that used to run up the river from Clonakilty Bay. Wrong again! A moment later an otter poked its head out of the water, saw me and dived again. On another occasion and after heavy rain (not unusual in Ireland), I landed a sea trout of 2½ pounds literally a few yards from my front door, fishing a small gold meps spoon.

We had a further encounter with an otter, this time at Sands Cove, where we used to go to collect winkles. There was a pile of rubbish on the beach in which Rip took a great interest. Suddenly he flushed an otter which bit him on the shoulder, but not before Rip had got a swift bite in. They raced down the beach and the otter ran into the water and dived under. As Jack Russells are not swimming dogs Rip just stood and watched, probably thinking it had drowned. Regarding the winkle picking, Edna and I used to do this in our spare time, sometimes with James O'Donoghue. We used to get paid five pounds per hundredweight. I don't know how many that represents, but believe me, it's quite often thousands! It was OK in a good patch when you could scoop up a handful of twenty or thirty, but picking them one at a time was a dead loss.

Clonakilty also had amazing bird life and amongst the rarities were choughs performing aerobatics over the cliffs. I also once saw a hoopoe in the woods. Ravens were a common sight and both yellow and pied wagtails nested in the walls surrounding the River Feal. We used to feed the jackdaws and hooded crows (those with a grey cap) on the roof of the lean-to shed in the yard. Of the raptors, there was the odd hen harrier and quite a few peregrine falcons. This was because Inchydony, our local beach, was a release point for homing pigeons flying to Dublin and all points east. Quite a few of them decided to stay in Clonakilty and as they are the favourite food of the peregrines, they paid the price! We also had hummingbird hawk moths in the back yard, hovering over the wild valerian growing out of the ancient walls.

The River Brandon provided good dry fly fishing for wild brown trout and the occasional salmon, though I never succeeded in catching one of the latter.

The River Argideen was a very good sea trout river and had a members' club. We used to meet on the bridge at dusk and draw for the various pools on the stretch. On arriving at your designated patch you quite often found it already being fished by a tourist, who did not even have a licence or permit to fish. Anyway, I caught several good fish up to 2 pounds at night. I decided to give it a go in the early morning and arriving at dawn I went straight to 'strawberry', a pool I had fancied, but never been lucky enough to draw. The first sight that greeted me was a dipper gaily bobbing about on the rocks—another first for me, as I had never seen one before. There was a smallish salmon, I reckon about 5 pounds in weight, lying at the head of the pool. I tied on the largest fly I had in my box, a size 8 Alexander, a relic from my Chew Valley days. On the third or fourth cast the fish turned onto my fly. Unfortunately, I saw this happen and it led me to strike too soon, pulling the fly away from the fish. I should have waited for the pull on the line. Another chance missed!

George Cole had purchased a house near ours in Connolly Street for his employees to stay in when visiting from North West Blanks in England, this being cheaper than putting them up in the Emmet Hotel. He asked Edna to do the catering for them, just evening meals and breakfast, not lunch. They left the washing up, of course!

In 1978 I agreed to act as navigator to Roland in the West Cork Rally in his rally car, which was a Ford Escort powered by a Lotus engine. Unfortunately, I contracted hepatitis a week before the event. I'd never felt so bad in my life and thought I was going to turn my toes up, as did everyone else. A local farmer took my place as Roland's navigator. Unfortunately, instead of using a pencil to mark off the corners as they were completed, he tried to use his thumb as a marker. Of course, the very first bump shifted his thumb and there are quite a few bumps in Irish byroads, so he did not have a clue if the next bend was left or right hand.

However, by the following year, I was fit and despite numerous minor prangs we actually managed to finish third in our class. For this we were each presented with an inscribed earthenware pint pot and a cheque for ten pounds. George Cole claimed the latter, as he had spent a lot of money sponsoring the car. We competed in a new car in 1980. It was still a Ford Escort but this time powered by a 2000 cc Pinto engine that was very fast. We broke the record on the first section but on the next section we also broke the transmission, so that was the end of that!

In 1981, things became even more dramatic. On the very first section we crashed badly on a 90 degree left bend, mounting the offside wall and rolling the car three times. We finished up neatly parked and upside down on the left-hand side of the road. Well done Roland! I was knocked out and later found a deep gash on top of my helmet where the roof of the car had caved in. Roland got me out through the back screen, or rather where it was before the crash. I was soaked in petrol from the tank and a spectator rushed up and stuck a fag in my mouth. I just stopped him from lighting it as I had no desire to end up in a ball

Me, Roland and the Escort. After the crash—West Cork Rally, Clonakilty 1981.

of fire. Then a lady from a nearby farm gave me a mug of tea laced with a large shot of poteen; this made me feel much better, as you do when you're slightly pissed. I felt fine for a couple of weeks but then suffered dizzy spells and sickness, so off I went again to the hospital where the consultant rushed me past the waiting people into X-ray. I got the result straight away and was told that I had a fracture at the top of my spine. In other words, I'd broken my neck and so I had to wear a brace for a month. To think I had been walking around all the time and working on an ocean-going yacht in dry dock, sometimes thirty feet up in the air. After this Edna and Mary, Roland's wife, would not let us go out to play anymore!

However, the next year I was briefly tempted to act as navigator to one of the local drivers, or lunatic, as it turned out. He had bought our wrecked Escort, fitted a new body shell and done all the other repairs. He took me out for a trial spin, which frightened me to death so I refused his offer. This turned out to be a lucky escape, as on a coastal section he hit the bank and rolled the car, nearly going over the cliff into the sea some fifty feet below. This time the car was a complete write-off and both the driver and navigator were injured.

At this time I was working at Spiller's in the main street of Clonakilty. They had three businesses, a wood yard at the back, a hardware shop, and next to that a 'fancy' goods shop which sold everything from musical instruments, sports goods as well as cigarettes, postcards and, of course, fishing tackle. The latter I quickly developed until Spiller's became the No. 1 outlet in Clon.

It was while working there that I met Noel Redding, lead guitarist in Jimi Hendrix's band. He was still trying to get the royalties owed to him. He lived in a large farmhouse at Sands Cove with his partner Carol, and they were so broke in the early days that he used to collect firewood from the woods at Long Strand and Carol used to hawk homemade jams and pickles around Clon. He also performed nightly at Shanley's Bar opposite our house, with Mossie Shanley on piano, brilliant! He always complained that the customers bought him pints when he would rather have had the cash. I got him special strings for his guitar and in return he would tune my instruments before sale, as I did not know the first thing about it. He had his house raided by the Garda (police) looking for cannabis plants in the attic. Noel said he reckoned that birds had dropped the seed and they believed him. However, he got some good stuff from somewhere! Carol died in a car crash in Cork city in 1990 and Noel himself followed her a few years ago. A lifetime addiction to drugs and booze, I fear.

At this time, Edna, apart from running two houses, was also taking in bed and breakfast guests. We had people visiting from all over the world. A young German couple, Willie and Heiki, became friends and they liked it so much that they came back the next year when I made Willie a rod to catch eels in his local river. I should mention that Edna had run a B&B business before, while we were living at Southfields in Norfolk. We had a very mixed lot of guests there, including Lotus workers, racing drivers from Snetterton, HGV drivers and hippies. There was also Jim, a regular, who was in charge of a gang making cages for broiler chickens. There were three men who stayed for a fortnight before Christmas and left without paying, which completely ruined the festive season for us; all attempts to track them down failed. Then there was Cliff, who worked for a local asphalt firm. His wife had taken up with a Staff Sergeant in the USAF stationed at Mildenhall and she had booted him out of his house to make room for the new man. However, I used to take him over on Sundays to give her the best part of his wages. I think he also paid the rent or mortgage, or whatever— poor man.

The shore fishing in Ireland was very good, with plenty of bass, flounders and pollock off the rocks. My best bass was only 4 pounds, which I caught at Ring Pier on my very first outing, spinning an amber rubber sand eel. However, I did manage to get into the 1983 Irish record book with a flounder, 4 pounds, caught on soft crab and again at Ring Pier. One day a Dr Featherstone from Liverpool came into Spiller's asking where was the best place to catch bass so I suggested Ring, fished on a coming tide. I sold him a few sand eels and off he went. He was back in the shop an hour later with a 16 pound 3 ounce bass, less than a pound under the Irish record—that's how it goes!

Through Spiller's, I made friends with a Mr Jarrold, a member of the family owning a very high class department store in Norwich. I delivered some rods to him and Edna and I spent a very happy day with him and his wife who told us they were thinking of moving to Canada. We always go west, he said! He rented a private stretch on the River Blackwater and caught plenty of salmon.

It was while driving back to Clon from Cork that I got the first signs of hepatitis that had put me out of the 1978 West Cork Rally, as I mentioned earlier. I really don't know how I made it. After a bad night and a visit from my doctor in the morning, I was rushed into hospital in Cork. There were seven hospitals in Cork, and during my ten years in Ireland I visited them all through illnesses and accidents. On leaving hospital I was advised, or rather told, to cut out the alcohol. This I duly did and, as there was no smoking in hospital, I packed that up as well.

As a newly reformed character, I became very interested in cycling again, harking back to the days of my youth when I was a regular competitor in time trials over twenty-five and thirty miles on the Portsmouth Road, Crawley and the Bath Road. The Bath Road trials were the fastest as it was all dead flat!

I ordered a bicycle from the local dealer, (he called anything with drop handlebars a racer) and had chosen a top-of-the-range Peugeot. This was always going to come 'next week' but never did. The same thing happened to Roland over a BMX he had ordered as a Christmas present for his youngest son, Andrew. Eventually, I got fed up with the dealer's lies and ordered a frame and wheels from Pete Matthews in Liverpool. He was the best wheel builder in England and I duly received a pair of ultra narrow high pressure rims and tyres, very highly strung and built on Campagnolo hubs. I had the lot sent over on the Shannon Vale van, thus avoiding duty. The rest of the bits I got from Hardings, the local lightweight cycle specialist in Cork city. The frame was also superb, built for Reynolds 53, with double butted tubing throughout.

I got quite keen and was doing about fifty miles a night in the very hilly country surrounding Clon. I also took part in several 'round the houses' races in which I did not do well. As an 'oldie' I had to race with the juniors, under eighteens, and, although over a shorter distance, they were even faster than the seniors.

I decided to have a go at cycling across Ireland end-to-end. I was going to ride from the most southerly to the most northerly lighthouse, a distance of about three hundred miles. This would involve an overnight stop, as there was no way I was going to do it in one ride, I'm not that heroic. I was going to attempt it as a charity ride for Cheshire Home in Cork and they were keen on the idea. Unfortunately, quite a few local people wanted to join in on ordinary 'sit up and beg' machines. I explained that this was not a club run; all we needed were a few fairy cycles and trade bikes to complete the picture. I gave up the whole idea which was a pity as I had already arranged a support car, spare wheels, and everything else.

Whilst still working at Spiller's I met Renzie McCarthy, who had a boat moored at Duneen. I went out with him many times and the fishing was very good. I had plenty of conger and ling up to 20 pounds as well as numerous mackerel and pollock. He decided to take tourists out for half and full day fishing trips. I went on the early morning radio to do the advertising. It all went well; the only trouble being that the boat was round-hulled and rolled like a drunken pig if there was any sort of sea running, resulting in lots of clients getting sea sick.

Roland also had a boat, which he purchased from a local priest in a half-finished state and completed himself. Our trips mainly consisted of catching mackerel, as for some reason he would not anchor up and fish on the bottom for the better fish. Roland returned to England and sold the boat to a man in Courtmacsherry, where it slipped its moorings and finished up on the rocks at the mouth of the bay, broken into many pieces. However, the owners managed to salvage the outboard engine.

Courtmacsherry was noted for its very good hotel. There was a cork oak in the grounds. These are native to Portugal where the bark is used to make fishing rod handles and wine bottle stoppers. This is all in the past, as modern synthetic materials have taken over. On the other side of Courtmacsherry Bay was another, even better, hotel named The Pink Elephant. It was so called because of a quartz rock in the bay, which was shaped like an elephant and glowed pink in the setting sun. The hotel was run by Bill Wafer and renowned for the quality of the food. One year, when Gill was staying with us, we discovered that it was the only bar open on New Year's Eve in the whole of West Cork. Not surprisingly, it was a lively night!

The Festival of West Cork took place every year in Clonakilty and the Wolfe Tones, a group from Dublin, would come down to perform. They specialised in rebel songs. Tommy Burns, their lead singer, would get on stage and ask "Any English in here?" This made Edna and I feel like crawling under our seats as we were the only English present. Anyway, Tommy came into Spiller's on the Saturday to order some lugworm for the festival boat match on the Sunday. We arranged to meet on Ring Pier as I was also fishing. As they were still sorting the boats out Tommy suggested a quick drink in the local pub, which was of course open as usual (this was at 9:00 a.m.). I was wearing my green cycling jersey and Tommy had on a red, white and blue T-shirt. He then said "Perhaps we should change tops!" I won the trophy that year for the greatest number of species caught—twelve. I was fishing from Renzie's boat with him and James O'Donoghue. It was a lot of hard work, continually up-anchoring and finding the most likely spots for the various fish.

I went to Timoleague a few more times, once with my assistant bank manager who had never fished before. I fixed him up with some tackle and didn't he catch a small bass of about 2 pounds on his very first cast! Whilst we were there a mink, an escapee from a nearby mink farm, came down a gully on the opposite bank, dived in and came up with a fair sized sea trout. Nothing but the best! This was all in the sea pool of the River Argideen.

Edna and I also went to Timoleague to collect a Springer spaniel bitch puppy to replace Rip, our Jack Russell, who we lost to cancer. Ross, as we named her, was very kindly given to us by the local vet who was a son-in-law of Mrs Scannell, one of our local pub landladies. She turned out to be an even bigger character than Rip.

I was also friends with my bank manager's son, Dave. He too was a keen cyclist and had brought a lightweight bike back with him from England when he finished university. We did a fair amount of riding together. He was also a very keen bird watcher. One day I was out on the marsh near Inchydoney when I saw what I first thought was a white heron but I turned out to be a little egret. I had seen many during my times in Africa. I told Dave about this and we cycled down and saw it again. Dave reported it to the Irish bird society and before we knew it we were snowed under with 'twitchers' from all over Ireland, as it was a first sighting!

Our daughters Gill and Sue came over for a week's holiday with Sue's children, Marc and Melanie. As Marc did not have to return to school straight away he stayed with us for another two weeks. I took him out in a boat, Justin Houlihan's this time, and he caught a small conger and a dogfish—he was thrilled. On another occasion we took Marc to Loch Hyne, near Skibereen. This was an inland sea loch connected to the sea by a narrow and shallow channel. It was very deep and contained fish of all species. The fish had ended up there as their fry and eggs were carried into the loch on the incoming tide and could not return. Grassy banks and oak trees surrounded it—it was quite an experience to sit on the grass and catch sea fish. Anyway, Marc caught a fine thornback ray weighing 7 pounds on mackerel strip, while all I had were the inevitable dogfish. We were both using lightweight fresh water tackle.

On another day at Loch Hyne I noticed small fry swirling on the surface and jumping. Thinking that something was causing this I tackled up with a small

Marc at Loch Hine with the fine Thornback Ray he'd just caught.

spinner and straight away caught a large mackerel which weighed over 3 pounds. It would have been another candidate for the Irish record book, but we had taken it home and eaten it before I realised this. It didn't even eat very well!

One of my last fishing trips in Ireland was to the River Argideen once more, this time to the middle stretches just below Shannon Vale. The river was fining down after yet another flood and I fished downstream using worms. I soon had a fine bag of sea trout in the 1½–2 pound range. Yes, I loved my sea trout fishing; in my view they give excellent sport and eat very well too.

New Year's Eve, 1952.

I am now confined to an electric scooter as I am unable to walk any distance. I use it to go to the local shops and on occasion to the local betting shop, which is in the same area. Mike, the manager, always greets me with a smile, even on the very rare occasions I have won money. How he manages to smile and grind his teeth at the same time I wouldn't know. However, he's a great lad and some years ago won the 'Manager of the Year', quite an achievement when you consider the number of branches they have; no names, no advertising!

Then there is George, a good friend of mine, who is a permanent fixture. Why keep on going in when you've made your first million? I suppose there's always the second! The only time he is missing is when Norwich City are playing at home as he has a season ticket for the Canaries home matches.

There's also Willie, the Flying Dutchman, and his very friendly dog. He originates from The Hague, which I know well from the air, as it was our main dropping area for food to the starving Dutch during the War. I mustn't forget our good neighbours, Val and John, who help us out with many things. We are fortunate in having them next door.

Last but by no means least is my family. I must pay tribute to Edna, my dear wife who has stood by my side through thick and thin, and there has been plenty of the latter, believe me. She really is a brick and does everything for me as my

Self with Edna, Gill and Sue, summer 1957.

health has slowly worsened since I had my strokes. I often feel that she does too much.

Then there are my lovely daughters, Gill and Sue, who are both a great help in so many ways. Gill comes up regularly from Berkhamsted in Hertfordshire to take us on day trips and outings. She also encouraged me to write this book and is typing up the pages as I write them. She is indeed my co-author and introduced me to my publisher. Sue lives much closer and we see quite a lot of her as she is always taking us shopping and to hospital appointments.

Melanie, our granddaughter has recently returned from Colorado where she was on a month's course and is now a fully qualified equine dentist. Good luck to her in her new career. We also have two very beautiful great-granddaughters, Beulah and Bronwyn, Marc's daughters. They are twelve and fourteen and feel the loss of their father very keenly. We hope life turns out well for them and that they reach their full potential without him to guide and encourage them.

This about wraps it up so I will close by quoting a few lines that I wrote some years ago for the 218 Squadron Association newsletter. Remember that as a tail gunner in Lancasters I always flew facing backwards!

Could never see where I was going;
Only where I'd been,
And now this life is ending,
The outlook is much the same.
I still don't know where I'm going,
But thank God for what I've seen.

Amen